THE
PREPARED
HOME

THE PREPARED HOME

How to Stock, Organize,
and Edit Your Home to Thrive in
COMFORT, SAFETY, and STYLE

MELISSA GEORGE

CASTLE POINT BOOKS
NEW YORK

THE PREPARED HOME. Copyright © 2021 by St. Martin's Press.
All rights reserved. Printed in China. For information,
address St. Martin's Press, 120 Broadway, New York, NY 10271.

www.castlepointbooks.com

The Castle Point Books trademark is owned by Castle Point Publishing, LLC.
Castle Point books are published and distributed by St. Martin's Publishing Group.

ISBN 978-1-250-27530-1 (paper-over-board)
ISBN 978-1-250-27531-8 (ebook)

Design by Joanna Williams
Composition by Mary Velgos

Photographs by Melissa George, except images on pages vi, 3, 6, 8, 18, 20, 22, 24, 28, 31, 35, 37, 40, 44, 48, 52, 62, 66, 76, 85, 89, 90, 92, 98, 100, 102, 116, 118, 120, 123–128, 132 (walkie-talkie), 133, 139, 160, 162, 156–157, and 160, which are used under license from Shutterstock.com

Our books may be purchased in bulk for promotional, educational, or business use. Please contact your local bookseller or the Macmillan Corporate and Premium Sales Department at 1-800-221-7945, extension 5442, or by email at MacmillanSpecialMarkets@macmillan.com.

First Edition: 2021

10 9 8 7 6 5 4 3 2

To my husband—thank you for loving me unconditionally,
encouraging me endlessly, embracing my never-ending projects,
and especially for waking up early with the dogs so I don't have to.

— MG

Discover the secrets
to prepping in style.

CONTENTS

Bigger Ouch!

Stock your home without sacrificing living space or style!

Hair & Body

Stay Clean

WELCOME TO YOUR PREPARED HOME

WHEN YOU HEAR THE PHRASE "DISASTER PREPPING," do you envision extreme preppers with obtrusive backyard bunkers or stacks of canned goods overwhelming living spaces? As you may have guessed from the book's cover, the approach of *The Prepared Home* is a bit different. Every page is designed to show you how your home can be gorgeous, calm, *and* prepared!

Throughout the book, you'll learn how to create a customized disaster readiness plan that works with your lifestyle even when your home is in everyday or entertaining mode. We'll talk about the items you may need, how to prioritize any purchases, and how to store everything in ways that don't take over your life. Because we thrive in stylish spaces that reflect personality, I'll show you how to incorporate your emergency items throughout your home in Instagram-worthy ways.

As you move through the book, we'll cover the different types of disasters, their potential impacts, and how to assess your risk for each event. Preparedness is a process and not something you knock out with one shopping trip (no matter how great a shopper you are!), so it's important to prioritize your needs and take steps to reach a place of safety, comfort, and style. You want to begin your prepping goals by giving the most focus to the situation most likely to touch you.

1 Because we are all in different stages of readiness, each section will start at the beginning—preparing for the first 72 hours after an event. In the United States, the expectation of the Federal Emergency Management Agency (FEMA) is that each family can safely sustain itself at home for at least 3 days, even if there is no water or electricity.

Completing step 1 in each chapter should be a high priority in your life. The good news is that none of the items you'll need to consider for this step are expensive or time-consuming. In fact, you probably own many of the necessary things already. But for what you still need to purchase, I'll help you be more intentional with your vital 72-hour supplies and bring it all together in a design-smart, organized way. Then you can relax, knowing that you're always covered.

2 Step 2 in each chapter adds a week of self-sufficiency to your preparedness. Once you've completed this step, you'll be set to stay at home in relative comfort, without deliveries or outside assistance needed, for 10 days or more. This is a great baseline goal. For most regional disasters, some outside assistance will have arrived by the 10-day mark, whether that be FEMA or disaster relief charities.

At this step, storage can start to become a challenge. While other books may show you how to fill every room with open shelves of canned goods, I'm pretty confident that you don't want to live in a cluttered space where you are constantly reminded of what could go wrong. Instead, let's make your home a beautiful respite from the outside world with cleverly organized essential supplies. Expect to also find a conversation about ways to invite calm and discover joy even if you need to implement a disaster plan. Our planning will include food you actually want to eat and things that give you comfort beyond the bare essentials.

3 The final step of each chapter covers longer-term preparedness. What if it's not safe to leave your home for over a month? What if you can leave, but there is no elec-tricity or water? What if there is a widespread connectivity outage and banking can't be accessed, so you can't make any purchases? What if the disaster is widespread, limiting government and nonprofit resources?

I'll be honest. I don't love thinking about those more extreme circumstances. I'm sure you don't either. But each time I add something to our home that will make it easier to handle any type of emergency situation, I feel better. I think you will too.

With a game plan and resources in place, you'll feel less stressed, more confident, and ready to make great decisions if you're ever faced with a disaster. And you never need to feel like you're choosing between safety and style—you can have both! I'll help you balance being ready for a disaster with being ready for a dinner party. That's because although it's very important to be prepared for disaster, we can't lose sight of enjoying the everyday moments of life along the way. Let's get started on the steps to feeling prepared so you spend less time worrying about worst-case scenarios and more time discovering beauty in your home and beyond!

Find calm and comfort as you prepare and manage risk.

First Aid Kit

Designating a smart approach to safety can be beautiful.

1

GETTING STARTED: PREPAREDNESS THAT FITS YOUR LIFE

DESPITE WHAT YOU MIGHT SEE IN THE MEDIA, disaster preparedness doesn't need to be an obsession that exhausts your time, energy, and finances and takes over your beautiful living space. You can greatly increase your preparedness in a less over-whelming way that fits perfectly into your lifestyle and your home's design. The key to this approach is knowing your household's unique needs and comforts and taking steps that work with your style.

Each of our homes, families, finances, diets, and regional risks is different. It doesn't make sense for us all to have the same checklist of items. Many of us don't have the money or space to buy food to last for 5+ years and then constantly replenish the stock as things expire. Instead, we'll start with what you have, and then strategically add to it in a way that works for you and how you live your life.

The mindset of progress over perfection will be helpful as you work to prepare your home for whatever life throws your way. As I write this, we still have things to add to our own home as part of our disaster prep and items for which I'd like to discover even more sophisticated storage. But instead of beating myself up about that, I embrace the comfort in knowing that if anything happened today, we'd be a lot better off than we would have been a year ago.

There are many obtainable checkpoints between being an average family without a current plan and being a prepping-in-style superstar. Wherever you are on that journey, let's move forward, one achievable step at a time.

Every little prepping step adds up!

KNOW YOUR NECESSITIES

There's a joke that meteorologists are really bread and milk salesmen, because each time they predict a bad winter storm in our area, the stores are emptied of bread, milk, and easy-to-cook frozen foods. Unfortunately, here in Oklahoma, the biggest impact of winter storms is usually power outages, so those frozen foods and milk are not on the list of what people should be grabbing.

While none of us should be stocking up on frozen pizzas the night before a possible power outage, there is still a difference in my necessities and your necessities. I need to have extra water on hand for our thirsty dogs and you may need distilled water for a medical device.

Throughout the chapters ahead, I've covered everything I could think of to help your planning, but make sure you always pause and think through any additional needs for your family. By shopping smarter and knowing the necessities of your own household, you'll never be part of the crowd rushing to the store right before a storm. Instead, you can relax, knowing that you're always prepared.

FINDING YOUR BALANCE

A practical preparedness approach is all about balancing the risks of different disasters and the impact of preparedness on our lives. For example, you could add another freezer to your garage to increase your storage capacity for meat. That would be a great asset if you need to stay home for an extended period or if the price of meat rises during a pandemic. But then, what if the power goes out during a storm? The stockpiled food would be wasted unless the freezer was attached to a backup generator. I'll help you think through those chicken-and-egg scenarios in each chapter as you make decisions for your family. You'll see your plans and essentials fall right into place for your situation and your home's design.

Prepping isn't one-size-fits-all! Tailor it to your tastes and comforts.

CONSIDER COMFORT AND LIFESTYLE

Any kind of emergency or disaster elevates stress levels. While survival is our first priority, it's also important to consider our mental health and physical comfort. As you add to your list of essentials to stockpile, don't be afraid or ashamed to add things that aren't vital to survival but will help you thrive emotionally.

Assess your own personality as you incorporate comfort into every aspect of your planning steps. This will impact both minor and major details of your plan. On the minor side, my stockpile list includes extra coffee, shelf-stable half-and-half, and a French press. I'll feel better main-

If coffee is your comfort, plan for it.

taining part of my normal lifestyle and morning routine with a cup of coffee, even if we don't have power.

For a more major example, you'll learn later that living in a tent isn't my idea of a great time. That means our planning process includes taking as many precautions as possible to be able to stay in our home. For others who love the outdoors and may live in an area where it's harder to shelter in place, it could be better to devote more resources to an excellent camping setup, which allows you to leave town and tuck away in the woods comfortably.

Whatever you find comfort in, you'll be glad that you considered it if you have to activate your plans. Every little bit of peace of mind and sense of home you give yourself and your loved ones will help in a stressful situation.

CREATE A PREPAREDNESS BINDER

Before you begin purchasing anything else, you'll need a binder and dividers. Your binder will become your guide for each step of your preparations. More importantly, it's going to be your go-to resource if you have to put any of the planning into action.

While any binder will work, I prefer one that zips to keep the pages protected if I have to travel with it. The pretty aqua accents help it feel more approachable, and it looks good sitting out in my office while I work on it. Even with something as simple as a binder, I consider the style as I plan.

Instead of feeling panicky and afraid to forget something if a wildfire or hurricane approaches your area and you need to evacuate, you can follow the plan in your familiar binder to guide you through what needs to be done before you leave. You'll also be creating a checklist of things you want to take with you, broken down by whether you need to leave very quickly or you have a little warning.

To get a jump start on your binder, make tabs for each category listed at right. For easy reference later, you can see which chapters cover detailed information on what to include within each binder section.

BINDER TAB	CHAPTERS
Our Family Plan	3
Medical	3
Insurance	3
Financial/Legal	3
Contacts	8
Inventory	5 and 6
Meals	4, 6, and 7
Vital Records	3
Evacuation	9

A preparedness binder can be a calming guide in an emergency.

You'll be adding to your binder throughout the book, so keep it handy. By the time you've made your way through the chapters, you'll have a great resource. Keep in mind that the contents will need to be updated regularly. Anything from changing insurance to inheriting any heirlooms that you would want to grab in an evacuation will trigger small updates.

This is a good time to pause and add a repeating reminder to your phone or online calendar. Schedule an annual appointment with yourself to review your binder and make sure the contents are still accurate.

FIND NEW STORAGE SPACE

Creating a plan and gathering supplies for a disaster is great. Then, what do you do with everything until you need it? The goal of preparing is to reduce stress and chaos during an emergency, but we don't want to do that at the expense of living in a cluttered, unattractive home.

Instead, aim to add storage in places that are out of sight but still convenient to access. You'll find specific recommendations throughout the chapters, but I want to get you started with four of my favorite ways to find new storage in a home. You'll be able to look back to these basic concepts as alternative space for anything we talk about later in the book.

Look High

In many homes, you can find excess space between the top shelf in a closet and the ceiling. Installing an additional high shelf to each closet provides brand-new storage for items that are not accessed frequently. For example, we have extra paper goods stashed on an added shelf at the top of a hall closet.

In the kitchen, consider dedicating the cabinet above your refrigerator to hold extra stockpiled items beyond what fits in your pantry. It's a great space to store extra food that needs to be inside the temperature-controlled house. Because that cabinet is generally harder to reach, it's good for items that you don't access daily.

Our home didn't come with any shelving above the toilets, so that space was another prime area to add storage. In our master bath, we used open shelving, while the guest bathroom could accommodate a full cabinet. Between those additions, we can now store a warehouse-club jumbo pack of toilet paper. If you're not already maximizing that area in your home, consider how it could be better used.

EXTRA
GOLD
Flour, Sugar, Salt
Coffee & Rice

Extra supplies
can be ready to
use but easily
stashed away.

Look Low

The area under the bed is a prime storage place for stockpiles. If your bed frames are too low, inexpensive risers are available for each corner that will lift the frame enough for under-bed storage bins to fit. With a modern, streamlined bed skirt, the bedroom can still look like a five-star hotel and no one will know you've hidden supplies away under the bed frame. If you use this option for food storage, make sure that everything is in airtight bins so no critters think you opened a restaurant for them in your guest room.

The floor space under hanging clothes can also be utilized in some closets. Low spaces are ideal for heavy items, like water, so you don't have to hoist them over your head.

Go Vertical

This found space is my personal favorite. Utilizing the vertical space on your closet doors can instantly enhance pantries and closets. Door racks can hold a variety of small- to medium-size items, from flashlights to canned food. The sturdiest option I have found is the customizable Elfa line from The Container Store, but ClosetMaid makes a more affordable option that also gets the job done.

If you have trouble with any of the door organizers shifting when you open and close the door, Command products are a great way to keep them steady without damaging your door. For example, for solid basket systems, use the double-sided Poster Strips behind the top and bottom basket. For wire baskets, Small Wire Hooks can be looped through the bottom of the back of the basket and then attached to the door.

Beyond closet doors, look into cabinet door organizers. They use the same concepts on a smaller scale—instantly creating more usable space.

Add Stylish Storage

While hidden storage is great, there are also beautiful furniture options that can add to the look of your home and provide new function. Storage ottomans and coffee tables now come in a huge variety of colors and décor styles, from traditional to modern and

Door racks create instant space.

everything in between. They generally have a removable top and big open space inside, ready to be filled with emergency supplies.

Narrow storage units can add a new look and new value to your hallways. We use an IKEA shoe cabinet in the hallway next to our kitchen to hold extra nonfood supplies like aluminum foil and parchment paper. It sticks out only a few inches from the wall and looks more expensive and built-in because we swapped out the handles to match our cabinet pulls.

In the short, L-shaped hallway to our bedroom, we are able to fit a six-cube shelving unit. Across the bottom three cubes, I use cute bins that hide disaster supplies where we can easily find them in an emergency. Do you have a few feet against a wall where you could do the same thing? Don't forget to style these units so they look like an intentional

Only your family will know what's tucked insider hidden storage.

part of your décor. Adding art, plants, books, or other decorative items draws your eye to the top and away from the row of essential items.

Now that we've covered a sensible approach to preparedness that can work for any household and a start to meaningful storage tips that open up new space, let's take a deep breath and dig into the various types of situations we could encounter. It may be tempting to skip the next two chapters and get right into the action-oriented planning in the rest of the book. For the best results, it's important to get familiar with your risk of each event and how concerned you are with each potential impact. Everyone has a different combination of risk factors and risk tolerance. Knowing yours will help you decide where to focus, so you get the best return on any preparedness efforts and feel at ease in your decisions and your home.

REDESIGN AS NEEDED

Just as you may renovate or redecorate your home with changing needs or tastes, always be on the lookout for ways to improve your emergency storage in both function and style. It's normal to adapt your storage over time as your stockpile and family change. If you need space in a kitchen cabinet to add a vacuum sealer for food storage, what items can you move from a shelf to a door to create that space? You may need room for diapers in one phase of life and then extra protein bars as that baby turns into a hungry teenager. Beyond practical needs, consider little adjustments—new cabinet pulls or labels—as your styles change. If you've redesigned your kitchen, it may be time to freshen your essential storage there as well.

Consider what risks could be on the horizon before they hit.

PLANNING FOR THE POSSIBILITIES

LIFE EXPERIENCES CAN TEACH US how vital it is to plan. While I've always been cautious by nature, my eyes were opened to the importance of planning when a few different disaster scenarios connected with my life.

Two years after Hurricane Katrina, I traveled to New Orleans to help rebuild homes for a week. Seeing the utter devastation that still remained and talking to the homeowners about their experiences before and during the storm was life-changing.

Later that year, we experienced an unprecedented ice storm that brought down power lines throughout our region. We didn't have power for days, and neither did stores or restaurants. It wasn't safe to travel because the roads were covered in a thick sheet of ice and huge tree limbs were falling from the weight of the ice, day and night, with cracks and crashes that sounded like gunfire.

Each day, the temperature inside the house dropped without heat and we realized how dark it is inside at night with no electricity. We had some flashlights and candles, but not many batteries. Meals were creative without power or refrigeration, but we had just enough shelf-stable food on hand until power was restored several days later. Other areas went longer without power, and we wouldn't have been ready for that.

In 2019, we had extreme rain and flooding in areas that have not previously experienced flooding. We learned for the first time that our tornado sirens emit a different tone for flood emergencies. For days on end, we alternately heard tornado and flood sirens as wave after wave of storms came through. We learned to read flood maps and realized that while our house is on higher ground, creeks that are normally dry can turn our neighborhood into an island without access to stores when they can't flow downstream quickly enough.

Each of these experiences helped reinforce my commitment to creating a beautiful home where we can still be self-sufficient in a variety of scenarios.

AN UNEXPECTED LESSON

While I was in New Orleans, we chatted with a woman sitting on the porch of her home. She told us her story, including how proud she was that her son had repaired her home after a contractor ran off with her insurance money. Then she invited us inside to see his handiwork.

My jaw dropped when I crossed the threshold into her stunning space. Up and down the street, homes were still in disrepair with the now-iconic spray-painted grids on the front signifying the house had been searched. But inside, this smart woman had prioritized creating an indoor retreat for herself and her loved ones. That afternoon, her dining table was set for a magazine-worthy dinner for six. It made a positive difference to her mental health and her family as the neighborhood recovered.

All these years later, I continue to think of her often. She achieved some semblance of normalcy and beauty amid a mess, and we can too.

FIVE MOST COMMON DISASTER IMPACTS

What I have learned about emergency preparedness: endless types of disasters can be covered by addressing five ways these situations will touch our lives. While each disaster brings a different combination and severity of impacts, it's reassuring to know that preparing for five different scenarios can help you handle almost anything.

Each of the categories below has at least one dedicated chapter in this book to help you prepare before a situation occurs, along with tips for thriving during the actual disaster.

Know what you might face before starting to stock.

DISASTER IMPACT	DEFINITION
Stay at home	Something is going on that makes it safer or required to stay home.
Power outage	The electricity and/or gas lines to your home are disrupted.
Loss of safe water	Your running water is contaminated or disrupted and not flowing at all.
Loss of connectivity	Internet and/or cell connectivity is disrupted, impacting communication, banking, and so on.
Evacuation	Something is going on that makes it safer to leave your home.

TYPES OF DISASTERS TO CONSIDER

Now that you know the five key scenarios to anticipate, let's look at the most common types of disaster and which scenarios will come into play for each one. In the next chapter, I'll give you some tips for determining which disasters are most likely for your home.

As you scan the scenarios, notice that in the majority of disasters, staying at home is mentioned as the top possibility. I hope it's encouraging to see how much you can handle at home if you make some preparations.

Feeling prepared can be a bright light in tough situations.

Natural Disasters

DISASTER TYPE	POSSIBLE IMPACTS
Snow/ice storms	Stay at home Power outage
Tornado	Power outage Evacuation (if your home is damaged)
Hurricanes and tropical storms	Evacuation Stay at home Power outage Loss of water Loss of connectivity
Fire	Evacuation Power outage Loss of connectivity
Earthquake	Evacuation Stay at home Power outage Loss of water Loss of connectivity
Flooding	Evacuation Stay at home Power outage Loss of water

Other Disasters

DISASTER TYPE	POSSIBLE IMPACTS
Pandemic/public health emergency	Stay at home Loss of water Evacuation
Terrorism	Stay at home Power outage Loss of water Loss of connectivity Evacuation
Civil unrest	Stay at home Evacuation
Economic collapse	Stay at home Power outage Loss of water Loss of connectivity Evacuation

Start your preparedness plan with the risks most likely to land at your front door.

3

DISCOVERING YOUR PLAN'S PRIORITIES

NOW THAT WE'VE COVERED THE DIFFERENT TYPES of disasters, let's dive into two other important considerations. How do you know which disasters to plan for first? How do you minimize the potential impact to your family?

I'll bet you could tell me what type of disaster you fear the most, and that it may change based on what has been in the news lately. As I write this, fires are raging on the West Coast, hurricanes are approaching the Gulf, and civil unrest is a concern in other areas. In those regions, it's clear what today's biggest risk would be.

But what about the sunshining, peaceful days when our setbacks include long lines at the coffee shop and an overflowing laundry hamper? How can we predict what could go wrong?

WHAT'S
YOUR RISK?

One fabulous place to start prioritizing is with your homeowner's or renter's insurance agent. An agent can help you on two levels. Insurance is all about predicting risk and your agent can help you understand the types of claims that are common in your region and the likelihood of occurrence. Additionally, it's important to ask your agent what events are excluded from your policy and require additional riders.

For example, when we started having earthquakes in Oklahoma, we learned that if our house was damaged by the shifting ground, it would not be covered unless we had already purchased earthquake protection. If our home was unlivable because of an earthquake, not only would the insurance not pay, but we'd still be responsible for paying the mortgage while living in temporary housing during repairs. The same situation applies to flooding—standard homeowner's insurance policies exclude flooding, and flood policies must be purchased separately.

Ask the insurance agent for a copy of the flood map of your neighborhood to get a visual of where water is likely to rise. For a quick look, you can also insert your address on realtor.com. As of September 2020, if you look at the map view of your home, there is a toggle at the top to see the flood zones overlaid on your neighborhood.

For other disasters, you can estimate your risk based on a combination of your own experiences in the town, talking with others who have been there longer, and some quick Google searches. For example, searching for "Tulsa Wildfire Risk," I found a link to a state resource that allowed me to enter my address to get a calculated risk.

As you think through the following questions, which scenarios are your biggest concerns? Focus your preparations on the most likely impacts from those events first.

DISASTER	QUESTIONS TO HELP DETERMINE RISK
Severe snow/ice storm	Have winter storms caused power outages in the past? How frequently?
Tornado	How many tornadoes does your state have each year? How many times have the tornado sirens been activated in the past several years?
Hurricane	Has your region experienced hurricanes in the past? How close is your home to the coast or adjoining waterways?
Flooding	What is the FEMA flood risk to your home? What is the flood risk to the areas around your home?
Wildfire	Is your home in a fire-prone area near open vegetation? Is your home on a slope or hillside?
House fire	Do you frequently use the fireplace? Does your home have older wiring? Do you clean your dryer vent regularly? Do you use space heaters or candles?
Earthquake	How close is your home to the nearest fault line? Is the fault line active?
Public health emergency/pandemic	Do you live in close proximately to a large number of people? Did your city's leadership and fellow citizens respond to COVID-19 in a way you were comfortable with?
Civil unrest or terrorism	Do you live in a highly populated area? Do you live near landmarks, federal property, or businesses that could be targeted?
Economic collapse	Do you owe more than you own? Are any of your home or auto loans "upside down"? Do you have cash on hand or items that could be easily converted to cash or traded? How much of your net worth is dependent on the stock market?

Keep in mind that part of disaster planning is to expect the unexpected. While it's important to use past events to help predict risk, Mother Nature has demonstrated the unpredictability of life, so use your risk assessment as a starting point and aim to be overprepared whenever it makes sense.

If heating is a concern, make sure your fireplace is up to the task each year.

HOW TO LOWER
RISK AND IMPACT

Now that you have a solid idea of the risks you could face and which are most likely for your home, let's get back to the aspects that we can control. There are some things you can do to lower the likelihood and impact of a few specific disasters before we dig into the items you'll need to prepare your home for a stay-at-home scenario.

Snow and Ice Storm Readiness

Tree limbs falling on power lines commonly cause power outages during winter storms. Contact your power company if you notice any trees on your property or in your general area that are hanging over the lines. If you're in a cold area, consider talking to a contractor about ways to prevent ice dams on your roof. The last thing you'll want to deal with during a disaster is a leaking roof. Have your heating system serviced before you use it each winter to make sure that there aren't gas leaks or other dangers and that it will work properly when you need it. If you have a fireplace, schedule a checkup for that source of heat as well, and make sure you have any fuel needed (wood or propane) ready to go into action.

Tornado and Hurricane Preparedness

If you aren't in an evacuation zone during a hurricane, you'll want to make sure you have a designated and prepared safe space during the storm. For most homes, this would be on the lowest level, in a small interior room with no outside walls or windows, which is also the best choice during a tornado. For storm-prone areas, a metal shelter will provide both safety and peace of mind. If you add a shelter, check with your city to see if it has a registration process to create a log of shelters for first responders to check after a damaging storm.

Whether you have an actual shelter or a designated closet, there are some items you can keep in the space year-round so you don't have to scramble to gather them when the sirens go off.

YOUR PREPAREDNESS BINDER. Make sure it includes copies of important documents.

A WHISTLE. If you are safe but trapped within your shelter, this will help emergency workers know you need assistance.

TENNIS SHOES OR WORK BOOTS for each family member. If a storm comes in the middle of the night and affects your home, you don't want to emerge from the shelter safe but barefoot.

FLASHLIGHTS. Check that each is functioning and equipped with fresh batteries.

A WEATHER RADIO will allow you to receive important updates, no matter what your power status.

A MAP. If you're listening to the weather radio because the power is out and you can't stream the live weather feed online, it can be helpful to follow the storm on a map. Make sure you can find your location based on the landmarks on the map.

A FIRST-AID KIT and any vital medication will keep you covered.

DIAPER BAG. Fill it with what you need to keep your child cared for and comfortable.

DOG LEASHES. Think about essential pet supplies if animals are part of your family.

CELL PHONE CHARGER. Ideally, also keep an extra power bank fully charged in the shelter.

BOTTLED WATER. Count enough for people and pets.

EMERGENCY FOOD OR SNACKS. Again, factor enough for people and pets.

DECK OF CARDS, SMALL GAMES, BOOKS. In some storms, extended time in the shelter is necessary and you'll be more content if you have something to occupy the time.

Secure your necessities and your home.

You can also take steps to fortify your house and minimize damage, such as adding roofing straps and garage door braces to strengthen the weak points of your home that tend to fail first. Consider swapping your windows to impact-resistant glass or adding storm shutters. Alternatively, you can have plywood precut and labeled for each window now to make installation quicker before a storm. Talk to your insurance agent before deciding on upgrades as some may even reduce your insurance premiums. Win-win!

Fire Safety Steps

House fires affect about 1 in 3,000 homes, and there are some actions you can take now to reduce your risk.

IN THE LAUNDRY ROOM: First, clear the dryer lint filter after *every* use (even between loads the same day). Combined with cleaning out the dryer vent (both the vent between the machine and wall and the vent within the wall to the outside), you'll greatly reduce your risk of fire.

IN THE KITCHEN: Along with dryer vents in the laundry room, the kitchen is a common location of fires. Most kitchen fires start on the stovetop, so it's important that food is never left unattended. The risk is highest with gas ranges and lowest with induction. Electric ranges land in the middle.

But what if you stay in your kitchen while cooking and a fire still starts? It's *very* important that you don't use water or a non-kitchen-rated fire extinguisher on grease fires. Instead of putting the fire out, it will get worse.

Remember that fires need oxygen to burn. If you open the oven and the marshmallows on top of the sweet potatoes are on fire (shout-out to my sister-in-law, who almost caught my kitchen on fire this way), immediately close the oven to contain the flames and limit the oxygen. Turn off the appliance. Using a similar technique, if it's safe to do so, put a lid or sheet pan on top of a fire in a pot on the stove and turn off the burners.

Your kitchen should also have a fiberglass fire suppression blanket and a fire extinguisher rated for flammable liquids and electrical fires. Keep them near the kitchen, but not close to appliances that could start fires. You don't want to reach over flames for them. Being prepared with these items could be the difference between having a scary moment and having a devastating larger fire.

It's simple to stock your kitchen with safety.

FALCON®
MEDI TAC
FIRE BLANKET
CE Standard: EN-1869:1997
SIZE: 47 1/4" x 47 1/4"
WARNING! This fire blanket is not adequate size for adult clothing fire. Made from 100% glass fiber!

Take a release tape in each hand and pull downwards and outwards.

Drape the blanket over the flames to seal off air.
Switch off heat.
Leave in position until cool.

CLOTHING FIRE
If clothing is on fire, force victim to ground.
Wrap in fire blanket, call medical aid and treat for shock.

PULL TAPES
TO RELEASE

MADE IN CHINA

A pretty basket can stash an emergency ladder to aid fire escape from upper levels.

Check that your models are up-to-date, in the right place, and working hard for you.

EXTRA EXTINGUISHERS: In addition to having one in your kitchen, it's good to have a second extinguisher on the main level of your home, near an exit. We keep ours mounted to the wall in the garage, right outside the door to the house. If your home has more than one level, keep an extra extinguisher on each floor.

FIRE ALERTS: The items we've talked about so far are needed for fires you notice quickly, but what if you're asleep or in another room? Working smoke detectors save lives time and time again. Check the batteries and test them every spring and fall when the time changes. Consider upgrading to models that are interconnected and verbally alert you to the location of the fire. Some even alert your phone if they are triggered, which is invaluable if you aren't home.

If your home is older, check the current fire codes for new homes and consider buying additional units to match the new best practices. Your local fire department should be very helpful in guiding placement if you have any questions.

EASIER ESCAPES: What happens if you're sleeping upstairs and there is a fire impacting the stairwell? Did you know you can get emergency ladders for upstairs rooms that work with most windows? Placing an emergency ladder in a basket on a bookshelf near the window or in a storage ottoman at the end of the bed is a stylish way to keep it tucked away until it is needed. One-time-use fire masks can also help protect your face and lungs while evacuating. Be sure to communicate the location of these safety items to age-appropriate kids and any adult houseguests.

The last step is creating a fire response plan with your family. This won't be a once-and-done discussion; you should review it semiannually when you're checking the smoke detectors.

Make sure that each member of the family can explain two ways to get out of the house in a fire and that they know where to meet you outside. Talk to children about the importance of heading directly outside and not coming to your bedroom. It's also good to designate a neighbor whom they can go to for help if they are the first one out of the house. Make sure the selected neighbor is on board too!

During your semiannual reviews, talk about age-appropriate fire response strategies, like calling 911 and stop, drop, and roll.

The last fire safety tip only applies if you have a home security system. My friend mentioned that they do drills to help their young boys know the difference between the fire alarm going off, which would mean they need to go down a floor to exit the house, and the security alarm, which would mean going up the stairs to their parents' room in their trilevel home. The layout of your home would determine your family plan, but it's important that everyone knows what to do in response to the different alarms in your home. Even if you don't have kids, do you know what you would do if your security alarm went off in the middle of the night? Ours malfunctioned around 2:00 a.m. and we learned how disorienting that can be.

Now that you have a comprehensive plan for fires, write it down in the Family Plan section of the binder. You can also include your security alarm plan and what each member of the family should do if that alarm goes off.

In Case of Civil Unrest, Terrorism, or Other Crime

If you plan to stay at home as long as possible, there are ways to fortify your home while maintaining or even improving the appearance. For example, consider adding strategic landscaping under your windows. It should look good and match the style of your home, but make it difficult for any kind of troublemaker to access the window easily. A dense hedge of thorny roses can be a beautiful deterrent. You can also have clear safety film installed on your windows to help prevent shattering. Doors can be strengthened without sacrificing aesthetics by using stronger locks and hinges.

Looking for a reason to redesign your landscaping or update windows? Think security!

Regular check-ins
with your binder will
help you live with
peace of mind.

THE BEAUTY OF YOUR PREPAREDNESS BINDER

IN THE FIRST SECTION OF YOUR BINDER, OUR FAMILY PLAN, take some time to outline how you plan to handle each disaster from Chapter 2 that you've determined is a risk. As part of the plan, consider assigning specific duties to each family member. For example, if you have two children and they go to different schools, who will pick up each child in an emergency? Assume cell phone towers aren't working and there is no communication. If you have to evacuate quickly, what is each person responsible for gathering? Start your plans for each disaster now, and then add to them as you read through the book.

IN THE MEDICAL SECTION, create an information sheet for each family member. The sheet should include any current medications, allergies, and information on any health conditions or treatments that would impact emergency medical care. This section is also a great place to create a list of both primary doctors and specialists, including their phone numbers. Duplicate copies of this sheet can be kept for babysitters. Anyone can find it difficult to recall medications or allergies during the stress of a medical emergency. Having everything on one sheet will make sure your family member gets the safest possible treatment.

IN THE INSURANCE SECTION, list the different insurance policies you hold, including contact information and policy numbers for each company. If you use a local agent for a national company, it's helpful to log the contact numbers for both.

Here are some common types of coverage to spur your memory as you make your list:

- Homeowner's or renter's insurance
- Flood or earthquake coverage
- Auto insurance
- Life insurance
- Short-term disability
- Long-term disability
- Supplemental policies (like Aflac)
- Health insurance
- Long-term care
- Umbrella policies

THE NEXT BINDER TAB IS FINANCIAL/LEGAL, which will include a summary of your assets and liabilities. It's not a detailed accounting, just a big-picture glance at your financial resources as well as the contact information for each account. We have two versions of our financial summary—one in our binder and one in our fire safe.

Organize and secure important documents in a fire safe.

The binder version only contains our personalized descriptions of each account, such as Melissa's 403(b), along with the financial institution's name and phone number.

The safe version adds our account numbers, online log-in information, and approximate balances for each account, updated quarterly. It's very common for one person in a household to handle the finances. If the unexpected happens to that person, the surviving spouse is left not only emotionally devasted but also financially lost. This list is a great starting point for more detailed discussions, and a helpful reference if the unthinkable happens.

Here are some account types you may have on your list:

- Checking
- Savings
- CDs
- Annuities
- Stocks/bonds
- Retirement savings
- Mortgages
- Car loans
- Other loans
- Credit cards

Contact information for any accountants or attorneys is also helpful in this section, along with photocopies of important legal documents, such as power of attorney, property deeds, and trust paperwork.

FOR THE VITAL RECORDS SECTION, you'll want to keep a clear, up-to-date photo of each person, along with copies of birth certificates, adoption papers, marriage certificates, driver's licenses or state-issued IDs, and passports. The information in this section will be used to prove your identity and help locate family members if you're separated. Include a recent photo of each pet, plus their vaccination records.

Now that we've covered how to minimize the risk of disasters and your binder contains helpful information to use in an emergency, the next step is preparing our homes for the five possible impacts we learned in Chapter 2: staying at home, power outage, loss of water, loss of connectivity, and evacuation.

You will appreciate
having a well-stocked
and organized food
supply every day, not
just in challenging times.

4

STAYING AT HOME PART 1: WHAT'S FOR DINNER?

BEING PREPARED CAN PAY OFF IN UNEXPECTED WAYS. Several years ago, my father-in-law had a stroke that temporarily disabled him from working. Luckily, before the stroke, he and my mother-in-law had already prepared their home for emergencies. Because their pantry and freezer were fully stocked, they were able to spend next to nothing on groceries during his initial drop in income while they waited for insurance and retirement income to kick in. Having that food on hand gave them peace of mind and security.

While family, including us, would have gladly stepped in to help, they are proud knowing that being prepared allowed them to remain self-sufficient. Since then, he has recovered and retired, and his golf game is better than ever. They've successfully and systematically refilled their stockpile on a fixed income. We all have peace of mind knowing they are prepared again.

If you ever wonder whether having a prepared home is worth it when you may never face a big disaster, remember my in-laws and the fact that having a stockpile at home is like an insurance policy to get you through financial disasters such as job loss as well.

Being prepared can help you through all the storms of life.

Most of the world got a crash course on staying at home in 2020. We all quickly learned how fast store shelves can be cleared of specific foods and, of course, toilet paper. For many of us, this experience was a beginner version of staying at home. We could still access groceries and even pick up food from restaurants. Going outside and driving around town were safe, and our utilities all still functioned like normal.

As you work through this chapter, think back to anything you wanted, but couldn't easily find, for your family during that time. Those items should be at the top of your stockpile list. Then, take things a step further and imagine the scenario where you truly can't leave your home or receive deliveries. What if you had to survive on only what you have in your house right now? How long could your family stay well fed based on your current pantry?

For this chapter, assume that you still have utilities, including safe water. In future chapters, we'll dig in further and make sure your planning includes extra contingencies for more extreme circumstances.

STEP 1:
THE FIRST 72 HOURS

For many of you, making sure you have food for 72 hours will be the easiest step in the book. If you're used to cooking at home often, you probably have enough on hand to get you through 3 days right now.

72-HOUR CHALLENGE

To check your readiness, head to the kitchen right now and fill out this meal plan. If something happened today and you could only eat what you have on hand, what would you eat for the next 3 days?

Don't forget that items will be used up as you go. If you write down cereal for breakfast each day, make sure you have enough milk. If you have one package of ground beef and write down tacos on night one, remember that the beef can't be used again for a different meal.

MEAL IDEA	INGREDIENTS USED
Day 1	
Breakfast	
Lunch	
Dinner	
Day 2	
Breakfast	
Lunch	
Dinner	
Day 3	
Breakfast	
Lunch	
Dinner	

The right containers help you maximize shelf space and fit whatever your household considers essential.

BREAD

If your routine relies on dining out, you go grocery shopping several times a week because of limited storage, or you're in a walking city and can't haul many groceries home at once, this section is very important. Make a plan this week to start keeping at least 72 hours' worth of food at home to meet governmental guidelines.

The 72-Hour Challenge exercise is great practice for how to plan out your meals in an actual disaster. Instead of jumping in and cooking your first meal without a set plan, you should spend some time figuring out how to maximize what you have on hand to create balanced meals.

Because ground beef and black beans are both proteins, instead of putting them together into one meal, could they be better used separately? And if you have a limited quantity of shredded cheese, do you want to use it all at once for nachos, or would you rather have it as a smaller portion for several meals? There isn't a "right" answer for these questions, as long as you have a plan!

What You Could Need

Your short-term food supply should match your normal diet. The easiest option to stay on top of this step is just making sure you're always 3 days ahead of your grocery shopping.

If you don't normally eat at home, select less perishable items that you won't have to replace as often. Don't forget to consider breakfast, lunch, and dinner as you plan.

Here are some items that are great to keep in your pantry all the time. Remember to customize this list to your family and focus on the things you would *want* to eat first. Ideally, you will eat the items before they expire, even if there isn't an emergency, so they aren't wasted. Just remember to replace them when you do that!

PANTRY STAPLES TO CONSIDER

- Oatmeal
- Cereal
- Granola
- Protein bars
- Peanut/almond butter
- Jelly
- Bread
- Pasta noodles
- Pasta sauce (tomato-based and/or Alfredo)
- Chicken cans or pouches (Perfect if you're not a fish eater!)
- Tuna cans or pouches (These come in a great variety of flavors now. Try a few to find your favorite before you stock up.)
- Soup and/or chili
- Ro*tel/canned tomatoes
- Rice
- Canned beans
- Canned vegetables
- Nuts
- Crackers
- Other favorite snacks

Use the staples lists as a starting place for your inventory.

FREEZER STAPLES TO CONSIDER

- Frozen fruit
- Frozen vegetables
- Frozen chicken/beef/fish/pork
- Frozen pizza/lasagna/potpie (While you don't want your entire emergency supply to depend on frozen food items that have to be cooked, not all emergencies bring lost power, so these are good meal options to keep on hand.)

Skip anything your family won't enjoy eating and add your own favorites to the pantry and freezer lists.

How to Store It All

Your 3-day supply should feature all the foods that you would eat normally and regularly keep in your kitchen. This is a great time to get your everyday items in order before we start adding to your food stockpile in the next sections. Having a well-organized food storage space will be useful year-round.

Start by removing anything that's expired or that you no longer need to free up space in your pantry or food cabinets. Then, group your food into categories. In our pantry, we have designated areas for the following categories:

CATEGORIES	FOOD ITEMS
Baking ingredients	Flour, sugar, baking soda
Snacks	Nuts, popcorn, granola bars, beef jerky
Pasta/rice	Noodles, grains
Side items/dinner supplies	Mac 'n' cheese, pasta sauce, dinner helper sauces/kits
Canned items	Soups, veggies
Condiments/fridge backstock	Salad dressing, barbecue sauce, mustard
Bread	Loaves, rolls, tortillas, wraps

For the baking ingredients and snacks, it's more efficient and attractive to remove the items from their original packaging to maximize shelf space. Ingredients like flour and sugar will last longer in airtight containers. Bulk snack items can also be stored in airtight containers, while individually packaged snacks can be placed in clear, easy-to-access bins or baskets. If we had left the different items in their original packaging, the shelf would be an overflowing, cluttered mess instead of a stylish space that works as well as it looks!

For your canned items, consider purchasing can organizers for at least one of your pantry shelves. They help you store more on each shelf while also making it easier to see what you have in stock.

Clear bins help you navigate the freezer maze.

Once you've organized your pantry and freed up space for the next step, you can use the same process in both your refrigerator and freezer. Remove everything and separate the items that are still edible into logical groupings and gather them into clear bins. For example, all our cheese is together in one place so it's easy to see what we have on hand. Opened items are kept at the front of the bin and unopened packages go in the back. Like in the pantry, we remove outer packaging from individually wrapped cold food items to save space.

STEP 2: PLANNING FOOD FOR 10 DAYS

Expanding your food supply to 10 days may sound more daunting than 3 days if you're used to shopping frequently, but I think you'll discover it's an easier adjustment than you expect.

Remember that your 10-day stockpile should be in addition to the food you're planning to eat before your next trip to the store. So, if you shop for 5 days of groceries, you'll really have 15 days of food the day you shop. By the end of that week, you'll be back down to a 10-day supply, which should be the minimum.

Keeping that in mind, you'll need to consider the shelf life of items as you complete this step. While your 3-day supply of meat and veggies will be fine in the refrigerator, the next two steps will benefit from your freezer.

What You Could Need

Can you double the quantity you keep on hand of any items you purchase regularly? For years, we kept one carton of eggs in the fridge and replaced it when we were down to one or two eggs. I realized that because the sell-by dates are always a couple weeks in the future, we could keep two cartons instead of one. The older carton stays on top, and when that carton is almost empty, we add a new carton to the bottom of the stack.

As you think about your 10-day supply, the easiest way to keep track of food inventory is by creating a restaurant-style menu. This method is a great resource for both disaster planning and regular use. We started using the system during the 2020 quarantine when we weren't shopping at all. As time went on and we started regular grocery pickups, we found the menu system easier to maintain than any previous attempt at meal planning because it's so flexible. We're not assigning a meal to a specific day. Instead, we have a menu of available options to choose from for each meal.

Creating a menu makes
food planning and shopping
so much simpler!

No more staring at the pantry wondering what to eat! You just look at the menu and decide what sounds best.

Start by going through your pantry, fridge, and freezer and writing down all the different meals you can create with the ingredients you have on hand. Separating the list by meal, like in the example below, makes it easy to count how many days you can eat at home without a trip to the store.

BREAKFAST OPTIONS	LUNCH OPTIONS	DINNER OPTIONS
Cereal	PB&J	Burrito bowl
Oatmeal	Tuna sandwich	Stir-fry
Waffles	Frito chili pie	Taco soup
Smoothie	Grilled cheese	Chicken & street corn
Blueberry muffins	Turkey sandwiches*	Fajitas*
Cinnamon toast	Sweet potato & egg hash*	Penne pasta w/sausage
Breakfast tacos	Chicken noodle soup	Mahi & roasted veggies

We have found it helpful to include simple options that we like to eat but tend to forget, like cinnamon toast for breakfast. The more comprehensive the list is, the better we are at making sure we're eating everything in the pantry. When items have lingered on the list a long time, we know we should keep less of that item on hand. Add asterisks to any food that needs to be eaten first because the ingredients are perishable and don't hold up well (or at all) to time in the freezer.

Once you've made your menu, count how many days' worth of meals you already have on hand. As you count, keep in mind that some of your listed options could be more than one meal. If you make pasta, it may be good for two nights' worth of dinner or dinner plus lunch the next day. At this point, you should only be counting meals if you have all the ingredients on hand. As you go, if you have recipes that need additional ingredients, make a separate shopping list and only add the meal to your menu once you have everything you need.

Once you've added up the meals, if you're at less than 10 days, make a grocery list to increase your stockpile. This can be done by adding totally new options, like picking up a pork tenderloin for the freezer, or by increasing the quantity of ingredients you keep on hand for favorite meals so you can make them more than once.

To use the menu and keep it updated, you'll want to get in the good habit of replacing any ingredients as you use them. Don't cross an item off your menu until you're out of one of the essential ingredients. Some items will perpetually stay on the list because you'll always have a backup for the ingredients. Other recipes that need lots of fresh ingredients can be added to the list once you've shopped and then marked off once you've eaten them. During an actual disaster when you can't restock, you'll be crossing off meals more often.

How to Store It All

As with the 72-hour supply, try to keep your 10-day supply in the kitchen and pantry as part of your everyday meals. As you begin keeping more food on hand, there are some extra tricks to help you maximize your storage space within your kitchen after you've implemented the tips from the 72-hour section.

One of my favorites can be implemented in seconds. Look for under-shelf baskets, which hang under your existing shelves to create new storage. In our pantry, I use one to hold a variety of oatmeal packets. One basket holds several boxes of oatmeal, and the packets can be stored on their side like file folders, so it's always easy to grab the flavor I want.

Organizers allow you to easily see what you have on hand.

We use another under-shelf basket for treats—like our favorite sea salt dark chocolate caramels. *Mmm!* Having chocolate and sugary treats in a separate confined zone keeps them out of our main line of vision when we're looking for a daily snack, but still keeps them accessible for days when we need a little boost. With these special treats off the shelf, I have room to store additional food for meals.

Adding shelving can also be a big help. We had a large gap over the second refrigerator in our pantry that became extra storage space when we added a simple shelf. While that was a purely functional solution, additional shelving in our kitchen nook perfectly balances décor and storage.

FORKS

SPOONS

COASTERS

WINE TAGS

BUFFET LABELS

VERWARE

Open walls can be
opportunities for smart,
beautiful storage!

In our home, six shelves span from the floor to the ceiling in the space between two windows. The wood shelves hold a variety of barware that was previously in the pantry. The clear glasses look great against the wood shelves, plus they're easier to access during cocktail hour. The bottom shelf is just as functional, holding nine matching containers of kitchen items that previously took up kitchen cabinet or drawer space, from coasters and buffet labels to disposable silverware.

Make it easy to reach for your disposables in both emergency and party situations.

Do you have any wall space in a kitchen nook or dining room that could be turned into chic storage? For a mixture of open and closed storage, a sideboard with coordinating shelving above is a great combination. In addition to glassware, wine makes attractive décor in a dining room. You can use wall-mounted wine racks, or place a tabletop wine rack on a credenza as a stylish accent to the room.

STEP 3: PLANNING FOOD FOR 1+ MONTH

Part of longer-term food planning includes getting creative with how you source food beyond your usual grocery store. For example, we subscribe to a local farm's delivery service to get a bag of in-season vegetables delivered each week. They're delicious and healthy and have helped us get more creative in the kitchen because the selection is always different. We can even add on products from other local farms, including dairy products, chicken, and beef.

Because the products are local, they won't be disrupted if there is a larger supply issue across the country. Of course, some disasters would affect them as well, but it's an added layer of food security to supplement our pantry.

Spend some time investigating alternative food sources in your area. Oftentimes, you'll be able to find small farms that sell specific items directly to the public. Try the farms along with small local butchers now to find your favorites. They can always use the support!

While they may not be as dependable in some disasters, a meal delivery kit subscription lets you receive fresh items for dinner. I wouldn't recommend counting those dinners as part of your 30-day supply, but if they continued operating, it would be a great bonus and extend your stockpile with meals from fresh ingredients each week. We like to keep our favorite recipes from the delivery services in a binder as a personalized cookbook.

Add a page to the Meals section of your binder with a list of the farms, butchers, or other alternative meal sources you've found.

Another food source is available right within your own property—growing a garden! Depending on your region, gardening could be seasonal outdoors. However, you can jar and freeze a variety of produce to supplement meals throughout the winter. There are also amazing hydroponic systems to help you grow vegetables inside your home year-round. If that's something you are interested in, keep in mind that they sell out very quickly during a widespread stay-at-home disaster, so ordering in advance is key.

GREAT GARDENING

If you've never grown vegetables at home, get started with this fun activity in advance of the day you may need it. Many varieties of vegetables can grow in planters, which is a super starter option before adding beds to your backyard.

Visit your local gardening store to find out what is in season and pick a favorite veggie to grow. Lettuce, cherry or grape tomatoes, and jalapeño peppers are usually easy-to-find options.

Research your chosen veggie to learn what type of soil it prefers, how many hours of sun it needs, and how much water it needs. Follow what you've learned to help your plant thrive. While each plant variety is slightly different, starting with one is a great introduction and will give you the general knowledge and confidence to grow more food in the future.

To get the nutritional benefits of fresh vegetables in a small space, try growing microgreens. They are a simple way to add a bit of freshness to any meal. Add them to salads, sandwiches, wraps, and even burgers.

We keep microgreens growing in our kitchen year-round.

What You Could Need

The great news is that many of the items from your 10-day food plan can just be increased in quantity as you expand to 30 days and beyond. As you transition to keeping more food at home, the easiest way to prepare is to follow a one-out, two-in rule when you shop until you're happy with the quantity of food you have on hand. Is your peanut butter almost empty? Buy two instead of one. Are you grilling chicken? Add two pounds for each pound used to your shopping list.

EASY TRACKING TOOLS

We keep track of our grocery list using the Alexa app on our phones and on the Echo device we keep near the kitchen so that we can add items hand-free as we cook. You can also keep a paper list on the fridge or inside the pantry door for easy updating. Either option will help you keep the refrigerator and pantry well stocked because you won't forget items as long as you follow your list.

Use the menu you created in the last step to continue tracking meals as your stockpile grows. An optional step at this point is creating a full food inventory list. Instead of relying only on your menu sheet, you can track your desired quantity of all the different ingredients that go into your meals. Some people find a detailed inventory list comforting, while others find it totally overwhelming. I use a hybrid system.

Instead of keeping track of a full inventory by ingredient, you can track the number of times you can make each meal with your normal supply. That will make it easier to count the total number of meals you have on hand as your pantry stock grows. It can also be helpful to add expiration dates to your list. For multiples of the same item, just log the earliest expiration date. For example, if you have three jars of the same pasta sauce expiring at different times, just include the earliest date next to the menu item that uses that sauce. Once you've used that jar, update your list with the expiration date for the next jar. Using this method helps prevent waste because you can either use or donate items before they expire without needing to manually look through your pantry. It's not necessary to log dates for items you're constantly using and replacing, like sandwich bread.

While the 10-day menu works well listing complete meals, it can be helpful to separate your dinner section into main items and side items now that you'll have at least 30 days of meals listed. You don't want the whole system to get messed up because you ate mac 'n' cheese with fish instead of chicken. Plus, being able to mix and match will help you feel like you have more variety and reduce the boredom that comes with meal choices once you've been home a while.

Keep track as you shop and eat.

If you're in a home that requires lots of creative food storage outside the kitchen, an ingredient-level inventory list can be helpful to track where you've stashed extra food. But it is possible to be well prepared using only the menu option as long as you're automatically replacing items as you use them and keeping the menu up to date.

As you gather more meals, while also continuing to eat from the pantry, you may find your menu sheet getting messy. A hybrid electronic/handwritten system works well. My menu is typed and saved as a Google doc, but then I print it and keep it in the pantry. Changes are handwritten daily as we shop and eat. I also write in reminders of anything we need to prioritize eating so it isn't wasted, like the veggies from our farm box. Every week or two, I update the digital version and reprint a clean copy.

As we go through the book, you'll be prompted to revisit your meal plan and make additions for more complex scenarios, like the lack of electricity, water, or both. Don't stress about those factors now; we'll make sure your pantry is very well rounded for every situation as we go.

FREEZER-FRIENDLY IDEAS

As you add food to your freezer and extend your stockpile beyond 30 days, be cognizant of the potential for power outages. If you don't have a generator or solar power, frozen food may have to be thrown away if an outage lasts longer than 48 hours. Think about how long you would like your household to be self-sufficient. If your ultimate goal is 90 days, consider splitting your preparations into 45 days of meals that incorporate freezer items and 45 days of shelf-stable meals. You'll be ready for any disaster that keeps you at home, even without electricity. In Chapter 6, we'll talk more about generator options that would allow you to keep a higher percentage of your food stockpile frozen.

I recommend keeping at least 1 week's worth of freezer meals as part of your 30-day supply. Whether they're purchased at the store or homemade meals you've frozen, having ready-to-go meals will give you a break from cooking from scratch during a disaster. Plus, they will be a huge asset if you're ever ill or just don't feel like cooking after a long day. We don't wait for a disaster to eat these meals; they're part of our normal rotation. When we opt to eat them, we try to replace them within a week, so the supply is always full.

Keeping seasoned and cooked chicken and beef in the freezer is another favorite at our house. It works well in a variety of meals, from tacos and burritos to salads and rice bowls. This approach is a great time-saver. When we're cooking dinner, we just make enough to pack an extra dinner portion into a labeled, vacuum-sealed bag and freeze. Take a moment to think about the food you enjoy regularly. Would any portion of it freeze well?

While you could also opt to keep all your food stockpile as only shelf-stable, ready-to-eat items, we prefer having a wider range of tasty meal options, incorporating fresh and frozen meat and vegetables. Cooking a delicious meal while enjoying a glass of wine at home can provide a mental break from whatever is happening outside your home.

Are you making the most of your freezer?

CHOICES THAT GO THE DISTANCE

As you expand your stockpile, you'll start to notice trends with expiration dates. We learned that most organic milk is treated with a different process than nonorganic milk, which keeps it fresh for a longer period of time. If we buy that, we can keep more on hand without worrying about waste. You can also get ultra-high-temperature, or UHT, milk; its special pasteurization and packaging process gives it a shelf life of several months. While it should be refrigerated after opening, it can be stored unopened in the pantry to save fridge space. Powdered milk is another good option for longer-term milk storage, but it doesn't have quite the same taste. For longer-term planning, keep a mix of UHT milk for drinking and powdered milk for use in recipes once you've used your regular milk supply.

While we don't want to eat the same thing over and over during a disaster, relying on a few easy favorites that we enjoy, like burrito bowls, and keeping a large quantity of supplies for them has been a good tactic to increase our days of self-sufficiency without stress.

Dry soup mixes are another easy shelf-stable meal option. They taste fresher than some canned soups and the packages take up a small amount of pantry space. You can get a huge variety of flavors to match your household favorites, from classics like chicken noodle or baked potato soup to specialties from every region of the globe. Before you purchase, make sure to check the directions. Some soups only need water, while others have a list of necessary ingredients to be purchased separately. For options that require chicken, you can keep canned chicken in the pantry to keep the meal shelf-stable. Serving one of these soups with a fresh loaf of bread would be a delicious treat!

Dried potatoes are a good side item to have in the pantry when fresh potatoes aren't available. Like the soups, different brands and flavors require different ingredients. Look for mashed and scalloped potatoes that need only water as your first choice, or if milk is needed, make sure you have some dried milk on hand.

THE VERSATILE BURRITO BOWL

In an emergency, burrito bowls would be a very common dinner in our house. They're easy to make with only pantry items but can be enhanced with many different ingredients, depending on what we have on hand and whether we have any other limitations, like power outages.

SHELF-STABLE VERSION

- Rice
- Taco seasoning
- Canned corn, drained
- Canned black beans, drained and rinsed
- Ro*tel or salsa

1 Cook the rice according to the package instructions. Season the rice to taste. (We use a mixture of salt, chili powder, onion powder, garlic powder, and cumin instead of premade taco seasonings, but you can adapt the seasoning as desired.)

2 Add the corn, beans, Ro*tel or salsa, and any other meat or veggies available. (Even canned chicken will work!)

Any or all of the following items add extra flavor and nutrients when you have them available, but in a pinch, the basic bowl will give you the calories you need along with some protein from the black beans.

EXTRAS

- Chicken or beef
- Cheese (shredded or queso from a jar in your pantry)
- Tomato
- Jalapeño
- Lime
- Refried beans

If you have lettuce, chips, or tortillas, you can transform your basic burrito bowl into a salad, nachos, or—drumroll—a burrito.

Don't overlook stocking up on condiments and spices. A huge part of staying comfortable in a disaster is eating food that tastes great. While survival comes first, you should plan to thrive on more than plain beans and bland rice. Look through your spices and general ingredients in the pantry and fridge and purchase at least one backup for each regularly used opened item.

Here are some basics to get you started, but it's important to make your own personalized list while looking through the cabinets and pantry in your own home.

- Salt
- Pepper
- Olive and/or avocado oil
- Cooking vinegar (such as rice, wine)
- Garlic powder
- Onion powder
- Chili powder
- Other individual spices

- Seasoning blends
- Honey
- Mayo
- Mustard
- Barbecue sauce
- Ketchup
- Salad dressing
- Soy sauce
- Hot sauce

- Syrup
- Salsa
- Sugar
- Brown sugar
- Flour
- Yeast
- Butter
- Baking soda
- Baking powder

As you near the bottom of any of these items, add the replacement to your grocery list, even if you have a backup in the pantry. This will maintain your stock on an ongoing basis without needing to keep the detailed inventory. Remember to rotate so you're opening the items that expire sooner first.

It's worth mentioning that you can purchase emergency rations of grab-and-go meal pouches, similar to military MREs (Meal, Ready-to-Eat), which only need water added. The water rehydrates the contents with no cooking required. The pouches

Keep herbs on hand by growing your own.

are generally rated to last over 10 years and come in storage-friendly buckets. Using this method, you can store a month's worth of meals in a relatively small space with no planning required. If you're extremely limited on space, and keeping groceries at home is not part of your current lifestyle, purchasing these ready-made solutions is a good idea. That said, it will be a huge adjustment having to depend on them in an emergency, because they don't usually taste great. But you'll also be much better off if there is an interruption to the food supply than if you hadn't prepared at all. Searching for "emergency food supply" online will help you find a wide variety of options.

BREAD MAKES EVERYTHING BETTER

Serving any meal with freshly baked bread will make you forget anything unusual is going on outside your home. Making fresh bread is both simple and tricky. Minimal ingredients are needed to create this delicious food, but dealing with yeast is different from anything else in cooking. If you've never made your own bread at home, try several recipes over the next few weeks to find your family's favorite.

When you've landed on a bread that everyone loves, print out the recipe and add it to your preparedness binder. Be sure to stock up on the exact ingredients needed for that recipe. Some breads use all-purpose flour, while others need the higher protein of bread flour. Some recipes use active dry yeast and others use instant yeast, so picking a recipe in advance will ensure you have exactly what you need.

In addition to bread, are there other foods you purchase regularly that can be made from scratch if you run out of them and can't shop for more? What about tortillas?

Homemade bread is a perfect comfort food!

How to Store It All

Now that you're expanding food storage to 30 days and beyond, you'll want to be more cognizant of the life span of your food. Proper storage will help your items last longer and save money in the long run.

A vacuum sealer can help keep food fresh by removing the air that normally surrounds food in plastic storage bags. We use ours most often to freeze leftovers and love that removing air also saves space in the freezer. We make a baked ziti dish that feeds at least

Don't forget to rotate your stocked food items!

eight, but because there are two of us, that would mean eating it four times over a short period. Instead, we freeze half, dividing it into two separate vacuum-sealed bags. That provides two ready-to-heat homemade dinners for our stockpile—yum!

In 2020, I was shocked how fast our stores were out of basic baking essentials, like flour. I knew I should keep extra flour on hand but that it had a chance of attracting bugs in the pantry. Our solution ended up working well for a variety of items. We purchased a large storage tote with an airtight seal that fits in the cabinet above our refrigerator. It now holds extra flour, sugar, salt, and yeast, so we can make plenty of bread and other baked goods.

When you place your stockpiled items in a different area, it's important that you still rotate them as part of your normal food supply. When my regular pantry flour is low, I purchase another bag, but that new bag goes straight to the emergency bin and the oldest bag from the emergency bin refills the pantry container.

In the space next to the baking supplies bin, I had just enough room to add an extra can organizer. This is a great space to keep extra beans, veggies, and pasta sauces on hand without overwhelming the pantry shelves. As we do with the flour, we rotate these items by restocking our pantry with them and putting the replacement items in the stockpile storage cabinet.

If you purchase something like rice in bulk, consider dividing it into smaller vacuum-sealed packaging so you're not constantly exposing all the rice to air each time you use it. We figured out that 8 cups of rice fit in our pantry container when we refill it, which meant that we could divide out five 8-cup portions from a 20-pound bag of rice. Now the rice will stay fresh until we need it and the smaller packages are more manageable to store in the stockpile container above our refrigerator.

Storing food for longer than 30 days is also the point at which you're more likely to look outside the kitchen for additional storage of shelf-stable food. Review the tips in Chapter 1 and think about the layout of your home. Can you add storage on the door of a coat or linen closet near the kitchen? Is there a guest room or office closet available? Consider

Basmati
11/2020

A vacuum sealer benefits food storage and freshness.

Room for a second fridge or upright freezer? Go for it!

using the top shelf as a backup pantry. Do you still need the hard copies of music and movies in your entertainment center? Reclaim that space for extra snacks in pretty baskets.

If you have extra wall space in the living room, entryway, or even a bedroom, adding a decorative storage cabinet can enhance the look of your home while serving as an extra pantry. Dressers are also surprisingly versatile for food storage if you can't find a cabinet you love.

With any food storage, it's important that the area you choose is dry, cool, and not exposed to too much light. While garages and attics are tempting, if you are in an area with hot summers, your canned food will spoil more quickly.

If you have space in the pantry or garage, adding a second refrigerator or a stand-alone freezer can be very helpful to increase your storage capacity. They're also extremely valuable around the holidays, when you may have more food on hand than normal. If you go this route, make sure your secondary fridge and freezer are just as organized as the first. Food should be rotated regularly so it's not expiring or getting freezer burn. Any new purchases should go at the back of the appropriate container, while you use the items at the front. It's common for a deep freeze to be the place where food goes to expire at the bottom. It's often never seen again until the house is sold or the freezer goes out. If you only need freezer space, look at stand-up freezers instead of chest-style models. The stand-up versions with shelves are much easier to keep organized.

Smart-home devices in living spaces can help you keep a running list of items as you realize the needs.

5

STAYING AT HOME PART 2: BEYOND FOOD

WHILE FOOD IS A VITAL PART OF PREPAREDNESS for any stay-at-home scenario, there are several other important aspects that are easy to overlook. From personal care items like toiletries and medication to home repair supplies, creating your own mini store of essentials at home will help you stay ready for almost anything that comes your way.

This is one of my favorite chapters, because the changes you'll make to keep more household supplies on hand will benefit you whether there is an emergency or not. It's stressful to run into the store, in the rain, after an exhausting day because you're out of an essential item. When your house is always prepared with duplicate products, organized in a way you can find them, everyday life is a bit easier. And who wouldn't want that?

STEP 1:
THE FIRST
72 HOURS

It's a good rule of thumb to never make it to the last of any product in your home—whether that be the last roll of toilet paper, the last trash bag, or the last pair of disposable contacts. Commit to restocking your household supplies regularly if you're not already in that habit.

Never get to the last in your stock!

As we do for our food list, we use Alexa to keep track of household supplies. Being able to add to the list verbally, in the moment we notice something is running low, has saved us again and again. I cannot even be trusted to remember to buy shampoo by the time I'm done blow-drying my hair. I'll never remember by the time I'm at the store. Can you relate? Now, I never worry about forgetting items at the store and shopping is less stressful. Whether you use an electronic assistant or just keep a running list in the notes app on your phone, commit to adding items to the list the moment you realize you need to restock.

What You Could Need

As long as you're in the good habit of restocking your toiletries before it takes superhuman strength to squeeze out the last dab of toothpaste and don't rely on neighbors for emergency rolls of toilet paper, you can probably make it through 72 hours with your general household goods.

However, it's possible that you will need medication, first-aid supplies, or home repair supplies after a disaster. Make sure that you always have at least a 3-day supply of prescriptions for all the humans and pets in your home, and that your medicine cabinet is always full.

In addition to stocking up on medication, this is a great time to check your stash of first-aid supplies. Whether someone is injured during a storm or just while chopping veggies for dinner, you'll be relieved by having a well-rounded first-aid kit.

You can purchase premade kits with a variety of supplies, or put together your own collection using the supplies in the "First-Aid Kit Essentials" list on page 76.

A WELL-STOCKED MEDICINE CABINET

For each of the medications listed, keep equivalent products for any children not old enough to use adult-strength items.

- Pain relief: Acetaminophen, ibuprofen, aspirin, and/or naproxen sodium
- Antidiarrheal
- Antacid
- Upset stomach reliever
- Antihistamine
- Decongestant
- Expectorant (guaifenesin)
- Cough syrup
- Cough drops
- Daytime cold and flu formula
- Nighttime cold and flu formula

Are there any other medications your family routinely reaches for when ill? Make sure to add them to your shopping list now. When you're deciding the quantity to purchase, think about how often you use the items in a normal year, as well as the impact if you don't have the medicine available when you need it. Check expiration dates when purchasing and choose the version with the longest usable life, especially if you don't have a strong brand preference. There can be more than 12 months' difference in the dates between similar items just based on how often they are restocked at the store. I'm willing to pay a few dollars more if something will be good in my cabinet for an extra year.

FIRST-AID KIT ESSENTIALS

- Standard bandages (assorted sizes)
- Jumbo bandages
- Butterfly closures or Steri-Strips
- Sterile gauze (assorted sizes)
- Adhesive medical tape
- Elastic wraps
- Antibacterial cream
- Hydrocortisone cream
- Clotting gauze
- Wound wash
- Thermometer
- Pulse oximeter
- Disposable gloves
- Tweezers

In addition to the supplies, it's nice to include a first-aid guide. Look for a laminated quick reference so you can easily find the directions you need. It's also helpful to stock rubbing alcohol to sanitize the thermometer before and after each use, but keep in mind that alcohol is no longer recommended to clean wounds.

These essentials will help you handle a wide range of minor home injuries with confidence. In almost every disaster scenario, hospitals will remain open to assist with major injuries. They regularly conduct disaster drills to make sure every department is ready to handle a wide range of situations happening in the community. Getting to a sanitary medical facility should always be your first choice, but if you want to take your first-aid preparations to the next level, there are additional products available—from finger splints to trauma bandages for major wounds.

If your stay-at-home emergency was caused by a natural disaster, there is a chance that your home will need repairs. Keeping supplies and tools on hand will help you keep your home dry and safe until more permanent repairs can be done. In addition to the convenience of already having the items at home, you won't have to deal with local supply shortages as everyone rushes to make similar repairs.

Organize your tools now to call into action when you need them.

HOME REPAIR SUPPLIES AND TOOLS

TARPS: Aim to have enough tarps on hand to cover your roof. They come in a variety of shapes and sizes, and can also be used to cover broken windows or other damaged portions of your home. During more extreme emergencies, tarps have other uses that you'll learn about in future chapters. In addition to tarps, plastic sheeting can be helpful. While tarps can cover windows, in some scenarios you may need to cover the window but still want sunlight to come through. Clear sheeting is a great solution.

DUCT TAPE: You can use this versatile item to patch any tarps that are damaged and to seal the gap between tarps when more than one is used. It can even reinforce cracked windows, screens, or siding until full repairs can be made.

WATERPROOFING TAPE: It's great to solve any plumbing leaks until a plumber is available for a proper repair. While duct tape can also work in a pinch, having a roll of tape created to conform to pipes to seal leaks will be an asset. Indoor and outdoor caulking along with a strong glue, like Gorilla Glue, can also come in handy for emergency home repairs.

SCREWS, NAILS, AND MORE ESSENTIALS: If you have to put your tarps or sheeting into use, you'll want a variety of screws and nails along with a battery-powered drill and hammer. If you have space in the garage, having some plywood and two-by-fours, along with a way to cut them to size, can be a huge asset if your home is damaged in any way. Keep in mind that the power may be out, so you should have a handsaw or battery-powered saw. Additionally, if there are any large downed trees near your home, a gas chain saw or battery-powered pole saw could be helpful.

Your tool kit should also include other basics, such as a tape measure, pencil, utility knife, adjustable wrench, screwdriver set, and pliers. Wire cutters seem to come in handy more often than I'd expect. We have a full work space in the garage, but the tools are spread out into various storage locations. I hated squeezing around cars each time I wanted to hang a picture, so I got my own pink tool kit of essentials to keep in the house. Over time, we've added to it and now it serves double duty as an emergency repair supply kit and my daily tools. It's so handy that 90 percent of the time, my husband uses it for indoor projects as well.

General safety supplies—including eye protection, work gloves, and a ladder—are also important. We like multipurpose ladders that are convertible from a standard A-frame for work inside the house to an extension ladder for access to the roof.

How to Store It All

Your medication and first-aid supplies should be stored somewhere that adults, but not children, can access easily. It's more effective to use smaller bins with the items subdivided by type rather than one jumbo box of medicine that you have to dig through each time you have a headache or sore throat. I like to use clear, labeled bins, because I can always see what we have on hand and it's easy for everyone to find exactly what they need.

First-aid supplies can be stored near the medication, also subdivided into similar groups. We keep the most regularly used items, like simple Band-Aids and antibacterial ointment, in one bin of our bathroom closet door organizer, and the less frequently used items, like larger gauze pads, in a lower bin.

Divide meds into groups to conquer clutter.

Large plastic storage totes are perfect for holding your home repair supplies. It works well to stand up tarps and plastic sheeting in your bin like file folders in a drawer so each size is easy to find. The other emergency repair supplies, like your duct tape, can be kept in the front of the same bin. It may be helpful to add smaller containers to organize the other items within the larger tote. Put a label on the top of the tote to remind yourself of anything that should be added to the bin before a storm. For example, we use our drill regularly, so it's normally on the workbench, but before a potential tornado, we should grab it from the garage and add it to the bin. Gather your repair tools into a portable tool kit that can be kept near the tote. Smaller hardware like screws and nails can also be kept nearby in an organized storage case.

One thing to keep in mind is that garage doors are usually the weakest section of a home in extreme winds, so you don't want to assume that items stored in the garage will be safe in tornadoes or hurricanes. Basements are a great place for supplies in wind events, but consider the potential for flooding and elevate your supplies on shelves.

If possible, create space in a first-floor closet for your tote and tool kit. The supplies and tools will be convenient for any home project. My favorite option is to reclaim a coat closet and turn it into an organized household supply closet. Ours has space for the vacuum, along with the repair tote, tool kit, and so much more that you'll see in future sections.

You can redesign any closet to work harder and stash your prep supplies.

STEP 2: PREPARING FOR 10 DAYS

Now that we've covered the first 3 days of a disaster, imagine needing to stay home the next 10 days. What would you run out of first? With many of us relying on weekly shopping trips, it's possible you'd begin to run out of some important items.

Aim to have an unopened backup for every regularly used personal care product. This simple strategy should keep your home well prepared for 10 days without any complicated analysis. You probably already know what I'm going to say next, but I can't emphasize it enough throughout the book. Tailor this rule to your own family. Certain products may be used more quickly and need more than one backup, while others take more than a year to use so you won't need any extra.

What You Could Need

Let's look at some examples of what could be needed, broken down by type. As you go through the chapter, make a master list of everything your home needs to stay functional and place it in the Inventory section of your preparedness binder. On your list, note what you already have on hand and the quantity you'd like to have as your minimum stockpile. Once you know what you need, you can make a shopping plan. It may be reasonable to pick up everything in one trip, or you may need to prioritize purchases over time to spread out the expiration dates and costs. Remember that each time you pull something from your backstock, you should immediately add it to your shopping list for replacement.

Your list should come from the ideas in the chapter, plus a visit to each room in your home. Instead of trying to finalize your inventory by memory, take your phone or a notepad into each room. If you go through the shelves and drawers, you'll be cued to include things that could be otherwise forgotten. Don't limit your list to only vital items; think about comfort items as well.

There's no reason we shouldn't enjoy a luxurious bubble bath if we're confined to our home!

HEALTH AND PERSONAL CARE

Medication should be the first item you gather in this step, especially if you have any prescriptions. Be sure refills are submitted and picked up before your current bottle has less than a 10-day supply remaining. If possible, switch your routine prescriptions to 90-day refills instead of monthly. This often saves money and will increase the amount you have on hand most of the time. Do the same for any vitamins or supplements you take regularly to maintain your body's normal routine.

Have you ever found yourself scrambling through old purses for the right feminine hygiene products? Make sure your bathroom stash includes everything you could need, then restock as needed each month.

Does anyone in your household wear contact lenses? If so, purchase extra contacts, saline solution, and any other eye-care products. As a backup, glasses updated with current prescriptions should also be on hand. For anyone who relies on glasses, purchase a second backup pair in case the first are broken during your time at home.

While you're gathering supplies for your eyes, stop by the toothpaste aisle for extra brushes, floss, and toothpaste. If anyone in the house has crowns, it can also be handy to keep a dental cement repair kit to temporarily cement a lost crown back into place until you can get to a dentist.

Always keep spare replacements for soap (body and hand), shampoo, conditioner, face wash, deodorant, razors, and shaving cream. If your normal routine includes other products, like hair masks or face scrubs, include those as well. Even if you're separated from others, feeling your best is always a good idea. Being at home is a good gut check of what you're doing for yourself, and what you're doing for others. Prepare your stockpile so that you can keep up the habits that make you feel good, and let go of anything you're doing to impress anyone other than yourself.

What other items do you regularly use for personal care? Which ones would you hate to run out of, even if you weren't leaving the house?

If you have kids, go through the same process in their bathroom. Depending on their age, it's good to include them in the activity. Teenagers may have different ideas about what is vital to them. Teaching them to be prepared is a great overall life lesson, and having a backup for everything they use may even avoid the occasional before-school breakdown because they'll never be out of their must-have products.

COOKING AND CLEANING

In 2020, I thought I had done a good job anticipating everything we would need to hunker down at home. A few weeks later, I realized I had overlooked a simple, but essential, item that I had always taken for granted. Trash bags were in short supply at our house and in stores. Can you imagine the mess if you were cooking every meal at home and had no trash bags? They got promoted all the way to second place on my must-have list, after toilet paper. Luckily, I tracked down a box before we had a total trash disaster.

On a similar note, remember that you may be using extra food storage bags if you're cooking at home more often. In addition to buying disposable bags, add some reusable silicone food storage bags to your kitchen. Some brands have sturdy, wide bottoms, so they stand up on their own and are even easier to fill than disposable bags.

Those reusable bags and your meals at home also mean you'll need extra detergent for the dishwasher and regular dish soap, along with laundry detergent and antibacterial cleaner.

Are there any other nonfood items you use in the kitchen or laundry room? What about coffee filters, parchment paper, or foil? Paper towels?

Consider your laundry essentials (and possible increased load) in your planning.

FAMILY NEEDS

If you have a child in diapers, make sure you always have enough diapers, wipes, and diaper cream on hand to last at least 10 days. Consider keeping at least one package of diapers the next size up as well. Onesies or other outfits the next size up could also come in handy. It never hurts to have a spare replacement for any of your child's favorites—if your dog eats the baby's favorite pacifier, being able to pull an extra one out of the closet will be a sanity saver.

Pets need your planning, too!

For older kids, involve them in the process. Ask what they would want to make sure they didn't run out of, beyond personal care, if you were all staying in the house for a while. Is there anything beyond food that you'll need for pets? Our dogs would revolt if we ran out of treats!

How to Store It All

Like you did with the 10-day food stockpile, you should keep your 10-day nonfood supplies easily accessible so items can be routinely rotated. To make that happen without overwhelming the house, it's all about decluttering whatever you don't use and then organizing closets, cabinets, and drawers to maximize space. Donate anything you aren't using and free up that space this weekend.

Extra personal care items can be stashed in a linen closet or bathroom cabinet once it's been decluttered. Adding a storage system to a bathroom closet door can instantly provide enough new space to stock a backup for all your regularly used personal care items. The same door organizer that holds our first-aid supplies handles all our personal care items.

Within the closet, under-shelf bins can add another layer of new space for your bathroom stockpile, just like they do in the pantry. Add them anywhere you have extra vertical space between shelves.

You may be surprised how effective the vanity cabinet under your bathroom sink can be if you plan out your storage solutions around the plumbing. Measure the space available on both sides of the pipes and any usable inches under them. Stackable storage drawers are great to take advantage of vertical space and make products easier to access. For items that need to stand upright, like spray cleaners, you can add a bin on top of a storage drawer.

Other items will fit on the inside of the cabinet door to free up drawer space—for example, extra contacts and glasses can be kept in clear containers attached to the door with heavy-duty Command strips.

If your home has zero built-in bathroom storage, consider storing your backup personal care items in under-bed storage containers. Switching to nightstands with multiple drawers is another possible solution. Use dividers within the drawers to keep everything tidy, and start with the most vital items when space is a concern.

Hidden storage is waiting to be discovered under your bed!

EXTRA BLANKETS

STEP 3: PREPARING FOR 1+ MONTH

Consider a mix of basic and luxury soaps.

As you gather supplies for a longer period at home, there are two things to consider. The first is simple: adding more of everything we talked about in step 2.

Look at the inventory sheet you made and increase the quantity of each item so that you'll be well stocked at home for at least a month. This is a good time to set your own personal goal. How long do you want to be self-sufficient at home? Is 1 month a comfortable number, or would you like to be stocked up for 3 months or 6 months?

Whatever the goal, add it to your inventory sheet and determine the quantity of each item you'll need. Having one backup for everything is a simple and effective start, but for longer-term preparedness, the quantities needed will change for each item on the list based on how often you normally repurchase it. For example, you may need more tubes of toothpaste than jumbo bottles of laundry soap. You may also decide to keep larger quantities of the most essential items, like soap. While we have enough of our favorite body washes to last 3 months, we also have a variety of storage-friendly bar soap. Some are scented and fancy from specialty stores, so they will still be a treat to use. I also picked up a 10-pack of classic Ivory soap that can fill in as both body soap and hand soap and even be used to wash clothes if our other supplies are exhausted. Since Dawn can also be used for a wide variety of cleaning purposes beyond the dishes, we also keep a few extra bottles of that dish soap on hand.

As you're deciding on quantities, it can also be helpful to consider what resources could be available in an emergency. If the government and charitable organizations are still functioning, distributing food and water will be the priorities. Because most household items don't have expiration dates, I can keep larger quantities of those on hand and know that we won't ever be scrambling for nonfood items during a disaster.

In the event of an emergency with some warning, use your inventory list as a guide. While you should always have a full stock because you are replacing items as you use them, you might decide that you'd feel more comfortable with a larger supply of certain items based on the type of disaster. Don't contribute to shortages by purchasing large quantities at the last minute. Decide whether adding one more unit of certain items will be worth a trip to the busy stores.

Also, balance your needs versus those of your neighbors. We already had enough toilet paper on hand to avoid the great TP panic of 2020, but when I saw a small number of coveted rolls at one store during my hunt for trash bags, I had a choice. Should I pick up one of the packages since they were in short supply and we would eventually need them? Or should I leave them and hope they were a small blessing for someone who really needed them right away? After some mental math, I put my hope in the manufacturers being able to restock the shelves in the next 30 days before we were in true need. I'll be honest, about 2 weeks later, I was starting to question my decision as shelves were still empty most of the time. All was well in the end when I was able to purchase a Costco-sized pack before we were desperate. Things go best when communities pull together in any kind of disaster, and being prepared helps us be part of the solution by standing back to rely on our preparedness instead of overstocking during shortages.

The second consideration for longer periods at home is items that you'll be fine without for 10 days but will eventually need, like supplies to maintain your home. Let's look at those next, along with some simple changes you can make to reduce the number of consumable items you use.

Don't confuse being prepared with hoarding.

What You Could Need

As you expand your preparations to 30 days and beyond, start by considering whether any disposable items you use regularly could be replaced with reusable items, like the silicone food storage bags I mentioned in the last section. Because reusable items are also environmentally friendly, they're becoming widely available. Switching to reusable items when you can will also help stretch your storage space.

SIMPLE REUSABLES

Here are five of my favorites to get you started.

MAKEUP-REMOVAL PADS: Instead of stockpiling the cotton version, pick up a set of washable pads made from bamboo. They often come in a set with a mesh bag for laundering and go right in the washing machine when you wash your towels. I keep them in two acrylic containers on my bathroom counter, one for clean pads and one as a tiny hamper for used pads. It's more attractive and convenient than keeping the mesh bag out on the counter.

Reusable items can fit well into your preparedness plan.

FLOOR-CLEANING PADS: Our dogs are constantly leaving cute but annoying paw prints on our wood floors. We were going through disposable cleaning pads for the wet sweeper at a rapid rate. We swapped to a washable version and now I don't have to stockpile bulky boxes of the disposable cleaning pads.

DRYER BALLS: Instead of dryer sheets, try wool dryer balls to keep your towels fluffy.

CLOTH DIAPERS: Even if you use disposable diapers on the go, it could be worth investing in cloth diapers and covers to keep on hand at home in case of an extended emergency.

SILICONE STRAWS: To me, iced coffee and almost everything else just tastes better through a straw. After a long relationship with paper straws, I made the switch to silicone straws and now love them. They're dishwasher safe and much easier to clean than I expected. I just rinse them right after use, especially for anything other than water, and then put them with the silverware in the dishwasher.

HOUSEHOLD MAINTENANCE

Items used to maintain your home are easy to forget because we don't use them on a daily basis, but we'd sure miss them if we didn't have them. I've included the following four most common items, but take a moment to think about any other consumable items that your house needs to operate properly. For example, if you have a pool or hot tub, do you need extra water-testing kits or other supplies?

HVAC AIR FILTERS: Keep the air inside your home as clean as possible by continuing to replace your filters regularly. Consider choosing models with higher levels of filtration because you'll be in the house all the time. The more expensive options are rated to filter out more allergens and even some bacteria and viruses.

OTHER FILTERS: Keep an extra water filter for your fridge, faucet, or pitcher, along with vacuum cleaner filters and/or bags.

LIGHTBULBS: In addition to having standard bulbs, make sure you have backup specialty bulbs for any important fixtures, such as outdoor security lighting or recessed lighting.

BATTERIES: Beyond the extra flashlight batteries you'll purchase as part of your no-electricity plan, you should keep a variety of other batteries on hand. When deciding how many of each size you need, consider smoke detectors, security cameras, remote controls, and children's toys and games.

ENTERTAINMENT

The early days of staying at home are a bit of an adventure, but boredom quickly becomes a real concern. When you're making contingencies for longer periods of time at home, staying entertained becomes important. While it doesn't make sense to keep a huge number of fun items off-limits just in case there is ever an emergency, you can put some of them to use with a few simple techniques to make sure your family doesn't get too bored.

Purchase smaller, entertainment-geared gifts for each person in the house well before their birthday. Things like new family board games and puzzles are great options, but anything the recipient would enjoy playing with is a good bet. On days when everyone is

Lighten the mood and make time seem to pass more quickly with some entertainment.

mentally exhausted from being trapped in the house, pulling out a brand-new surprise can lighten the mood. Go ahead and gift any unopened items at the next appropriate holiday, and then replace them in your secret gift stash with something for the next year. Using this approach will make sure your kids never outgrow the gifts you have stowed away.

You can also create a gift closet of age-appropriate gifts for each child's classmates. Normally, these will be the items you'll bring to those never-ending birthday parties. You'll save time before each party by having your child shop the closet for their friend instead of taking a trip to the store. If you're ever at home for an extended period, you could come up with a system for your kids to earn toys from that closet.

Don't forget your pets when you're thinking about entertainment. If they have anything in particular that they keep themselves entertained with, like tennis balls or certain bones, make sure they have a stockpile too! As I write this, one of our dogs is chomping on his favorite bone and reminding me that it's almost ready to be replaced.

For anyone in the house who enjoys reading, figure out how many books they usually read per month and make sure they always have at least that many unread books on hand. As with everything else in our system, we're constantly reading from our book stash and then adding to it so it's never depleted. As long as the electricity and internet are functioning, Kindles are a great option to access endless books. We keep a mix of electronic and paper books to give us an easy escape and mental break from any disaster.

Are there any other items you would need to be safe and happy at home for an extended period of time? What about exercise equipment to keep up your gym routine at home?

GARDENING SUPPLIES

If you think you'd start or expand a vegetable garden during a stay-at-home emergency, make sure you have the supplies needed for creating and maintaining the garden. Don't forget related necessities for food storage for anything that won't be consumed right away. In 2020, canning jars and supplies were in huge demand and totally unavailable for weeks on end. Some foods require pressure canning while others can be sealed in a water bath using a large stockpot, so it's important to research in advance and have everything you need on hand if you're planning on gardening.

How to Store It All

When it comes to storing household supplies beyond 30 days, you'll need a bit more space. As you make your storage plan, be mindful of how often you'll need to access each item and how easy it will be to find. Don't store shampoo in five different locations. If only one spare bottle will fit in your master bathroom, keep any extras together in one place. It can be helpful to note the location of each group of items on your inventory list if you're tucking things away under various beds.

It seems obvious to me now, but it took me a while to realize I should be better utilizing the space in our guest bathroom. We keep travel-size toiletries in one of the drawers for overnight guests, but the space under the vanity is perfect for other items. Our laundry room has limited cabinet space, so extra laundry detergent, dish soap, and cleaning supplies can be stashed out of sight under the guest bathroom vanity.

In Chapter 1, I mentioned adding a cabinet above the toilet in a guest bathroom. It has been the perfect place to group all the hand soap and hand sanitizer in our house. Now I

Life is short. Buy the shoes.

Don't be afraid to have a little fun with your storage!

always know where to find it and how much we have without searching for soap under multiple sinks. On the middle shelf, I added bins for extra feminine hygiene products, which left the top shelf to hold 20 rolls of toilet paper. It's functional, and it looks great!

You can also reevaluate the use of each closet in your home. If you have a coat closet, consider switching to a coat rack in the entryway and having shelves added to the closet

Our coat closet works harder as a transformed supply storeroom.

to create a dedicated storeroom for your home. Because you'll be adding the shelves, you can customize the closet to fit exactly what you need to store. For example, make sure there is a section to hold tall items like HVAC filters. Don't forget to add a door organizer to give yourself even more room!

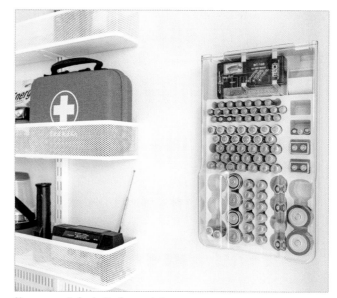

Never search for batteries again!

For batteries, order a wall-mounted battery organizer to tuck into a closet or laundry room. You'll always be able to see what batteries you have available and when you need to restock, and you'll always be able to find the right battery when you need it, whether that be on Christmas morning or during a power outage.

Use garage or attic shelving and clearly labeled bins to contain any extra supplies that aren't temperature-sensitive, like canning tools and supplies. While I lived 39 years without considering the need to keep extra toilet paper in a storage tote, 2020 made that seem like a great idea. In future chapters, you'll find more items to add to other storage totes on this shelving.

If you will be purchasing new shelving for your disaster supplies, make a list of the groups of items you need to store before shopping. This will help you determine what size bins will be best, and how large the shelves need to be to accommodate them. Don't assume that the biggest bins you can find are the best choice. It will be much easier to keep your storage tidy and functional with more logical groupings in smaller bins instead of having fewer very large totes with jumbled contents.

No power? No problem if you've planned ahead for light sources, cooking options, and more!

6

PREPARING FOR POWER OUTAGES

WHEN POWER TO OUR HOME IS DISRUPTED, everything in our normal routine is instantly disturbed. We lose lighting, temperature control, food storage and preparation appliances, and—perhaps most impactful these days—our home internet! When this outage happens unexpectedly, it can be scary, especially at night. If you've already prepared for the possibility of a major power outage, you'll feel more in control and know what to do if the house is suddenly dark.

In addition to making sure your functional needs are met, we'll look at ways to make your time without power more comfortable year-round. That includes several options to consider to make your home self-sufficient in an outage with backup power supplies or generators.

STEP 1:
THE FIRST 72 HOURS

Before you do anything else in this chapter, it can be helpful to enroll in text notifications from your power company if available. It's easier to plan meals and activities if you're getting updates on estimated repair time lines.

Next, think about your household's power usage. Is any of it vital for short-term survival—for example, essential medical devices that plug in or medication that has to remain at a set temperature? If so, the generator options talked about later in this chapter may need to be moved up to your 72-hour planning step.

What You Could Need

For households without special medical needs, when the power goes out, your largest concerns the first 3 days will be lighting, food, communication, and comfort. Let's take a look at preparing for each of those challenges.

LIGHTING

One glorious day, I realized that purchasing beautiful scented candles wasn't just an indulgence. It's smart disaster planning! Why have a closetful of plain emergency candles that you only use in a disaster when you could have a

Solar-powered lights add security.

houseful of beautiful décor all the time? And if I'm feeling stressed during a disaster, my favorite scents give me comfort and make things feel a bit more normal.

In addition to the candles, it's important to have a variety of flashlights and replacement batteries. At a minimum, pick up a small headlamp, a bright lantern, and a traditional beam-style flashlight for each person in your household. Whenever there is a power outage, we end up using both candlelight and flashlights. It works well to keep a lantern-style light (turned off) in a central location near your burning candles. When someone needs to go to the bathroom, they can turn on the lantern and take it with them. Headlamps are ideal for reading and doing other tasks that require more direct light. Just remember to stock up on lots of batteries for them.

While lighting inside the house is the priority, your exterior lighting will also be out, which can be a security risk. It also makes it harder to see your dogs during nighttime potty breaks. Adding solar-powered security lights around the perimeter of your home in addition to your regular landscape lighting can solve both problems at once. Prioritize installation around doors and easily accessible windows. We always hope that no one is burglarized, but if your home is lit up while others are still dark, it will look like less of a target.

FOOD

Deciding what to do with your cold food during a power outage can be tricky. Ideally, you shouldn't open the doors to the fridge or freezer so everything inside will remain at safe temperatures as long as possible. If you have confirmation that there will be a prolonged outage, it can be better to consume the food while it's still good. It's still important to limit how many times the fridge and freezer doors are opened because the temperature inside will rise faster with each opening. If you've been waiting for a special occasion to grill a high-end steak, go ahead and enjoy it. Rather than letting additional meat go to waste, consider grilling it for neighbors who may not have been as prepared.

Grills and camp stoves can be lifesavers for whipping up hot meals when the power goes out.

If you're able to get ice, you can move your items to coolers filled with ice to keep them at a safe temperature (under 40°F for refrigerated items). Is this an excuse to upgrade to a high-end cooler that keeps ice for several days? Maybe!

If you have a gas stove, you're in luck and should still be able to prepare meals. For those with electric and induction ranges, you'll need to rely on foods that can be enjoyed without cooking or use alternative cooking sources. Your barbecue grill can be an asset. Because we have an induction range in the kitchen that requires electricity, we keep a gas grill with a side burner outside. It's great for everything from heating soups and cooking rice to boiling water for a French press. Cast-iron pans are also handy because they can be used directly on your normal grill grates if you don't have a side burner. They could even be used over a firepit if necessary!

If you don't have room for an outdoor grill, pick up a small camp stove and the related fuel. Just keep in mind that these should still be used outdoors. Pull out your menu and make sure your shelf-stable food supply includes at least 72 hours' worth of items that can be eaten without electricity, like the tuna or chicken pouches.

COMMUNICATION

Sometimes the power goes out before the most damaging parts of a storm have even arrived. It's vital for every house to have a weather radio to alert you to severe weather. You'll get updates via the radio if you lose power to your TV. In addition to having the radio, I recommend downloading a weather radar app for your phone that will show watches and warnings for your GPS location. When you're in a severe weather pattern, you don't want to be caught off guard by a follow-up storm because you lost power during the first round.

Portable power banks for phones and tablets can help save your sanity when the power is out but the cell towers are still working. Look for a model that can recharge your phone several times, and consider keeping one for each family member. We purchased ours for travel and long days away from a hotel during conferences, but we also keep them charged all the time for emergencies. In addition, you should have car chargers for your phones. Anytime you're driving during the power outage, make sure your phone is being charged.

A multipurpose hand-crank flashlight, radio, phone charger unit can come in handy. While you won't be able to fully recharge your phone, you should be able to generate enough power for emergency calls. The options with small solar panels are even more convenient because you can recharge them during the day.

COMFORT

Depending on your climate, the loss of your heater or air conditioner can make things quite uncomfortable. In many regions, you'll be able to maintain at least a semicomfortable temperature for the first 3 days if your home is energy-efficient. Increasing your attic insulation and upgrading weather stripping around doors and windows can help your home maintain its temperature even longer.

Use window coverings to your advantage. In the hot summer, closing blinds and curtains can help keep your house cool during the day. Do the opposite in the winter and close the curtains at night to add a layer of insulation between the cold window glass and your room. If your windows don't currently have screens, consider adding them so you can sleep with the windows open if you don't have power in the summer.

If you have a wood-burning fireplace, consider signing up for a maintenance plan with your local chimney sweep so your fireplace will always be safe and ready. In cool months, make sure you have enough dry and seasoned firewood on hand and ready to go to last throughout the cold season.

Keep extra clean, warm blankets for each bed in your home. Merino wool, fleece, and down are all good choices. Layering more than one blanket will make all the difference in how well you're able to sleep in cold weather. Blankets can get a bit musty when they're packed away for summer, so be sure to proactively wash them at the beginning of each winter so they're ready and pleasant to use if you need them unexpectedly. If you have sleeping bags rated for extreme temperatures, you could use them on your beds instead of extra blankets.

Depending on your climate, consider battery-powered fans and heaters. The more powerful versions use 18-volt batteries, like those used by cordless tools. These fans and heaters won't replace your HVAC, but they can make a room more comfortable. Keep in mind that these batteries will need to be recharged, so they're not an ideal solution in every circumstance. You can get creative though—maybe a friend, family member, or workplace still has power and you can recharge during the day and still stay in your own home at night.

Cold climates call for clean, warm blanket reserves.

How to Store It All

At least one of your flashlights should be somewhere easily accessible from your bed in case of an overnight outage. We have a hand-crank model in one of our nightstands, so we know we'll always have some light, even if the batteries are unexpectedly dead. We also keep a lantern and headlamps in our tornado shelter all the time. The rest of the flashlights are in the cube organizer in the hallway next to the bedroom. You can see it on the cover of this book. In that same hallway, we've swapped out one of our electrical sockets for an emergency night-light. It automatically lights up in the dark and has battery backup so that it will still be lit during a power outage.

Install emergency night-lights in key areas throughout your house.

As for candles, we have quite a few spread throughout the house as part of the décor. Additional candles are kept in a cup and mug storage box. It has 12 padded sections, so glass candles don't bump each other. It's easy to see all of our options, whether we're pulling one out for normal use or during an emergency. If you tend to use taller candles, look for similar wineglass storage boxes instead.

A mug storage box gently holds a candle stock.

Your communication items should be easy to store. Because we have weather radar apps on our phone, we rely on those before a storm. We then keep the separate weather radio with our supplies in the tornado shelter for use in case the cell phone towers are damaged. The cell phone charging blocks live in a bin on my office shelf so I can check them and recharge as needed. Before a potential storm, I move them into the shelter with us at the same time I add my purse and my husband's wallet. Anytime the chance of tornadic storms is high, we keep an eye on the radar and add things to the shelter before the point that we'd have to take cover. If the threat becomes imminent, we only have to get ourselves and our dogs to safety and aren't rushing around trying to grab anything else.

For the cooking items like camp stoves and comfort items like battery-controlled fans, keep anything you won't use regularly in a labeled bin on your designated shelving. Anything flammable or explosive, like fuel canisters, should be stored separately in a temperature-controlled area.

STEP 2:
PREPARING FOR 10 DAYS

Longer-term outages can become a bit more uncomfortable unless you already love camping. While extended outages are uncommon in the US, they do still happen. In August 2020, a storm ripped across Iowa, and a week later, 75,000 households were still without power. During Hurricane Sandy, some areas were left without power for a full 2 weeks, and after Hurricane Katrina, the power loss was even more extreme. If you're in a rural area, keep in mind that it may take crews even longer to repair the lines reaching your home, so you should plan accordingly.

What You Could Need

Without a generator, at this point you won't be able to use any of the food in your fridge or freezer. Look back at your menu. How many days' worth of meals can you still make without electricity? Consider adding more shelf-stable, no-cooking-required meals to your food stockpile. Keeping a variety of snacks on hand can also add necessary calories and variety to your days if you think your meals will be a bit boring or repetitive during a longer outage.

To make each meal tastier, you can stock up on single-serve shelf-stable condiments. Mayo, mustard, and salad dressing packets will improve the taste of sandwiches and

PREPARED WITH A NUTRIENT BOOST

If you didn't already stock up on a high-quality multivitamin during your stay-at-home planning, add some to your stash if you anticipate eating a smaller variety of foods during a power outage. You don't want to become deficient in any essential nutrients during a disaster. Although it's mostly associated with pirates and sailors in times past, scurvy is still a concern if you have a sustained shortage of vitamin C.

Plan for all the little things that bring comfort to your day.

wraps made with canned tuna or chicken. Designate a bin in the pantry for leftover condiments you receive with take-out meals from restaurants to add even more variety. If you're like me and have no intention of giving up your morning coffee no matter what is happening outside your home, don't forget to add single-serve half-and-half or creamer to your pantry.

Additional propane for your grill may be needed if you're regularly using it to cook meals from your pantry, like boiling noodles and heating pasta sauce. Extra propane has very limited storage options for safety, so we don't keep an extra tank all the time. However, in an outage that isn't anticipated to be resolved quickly, our first purchase would be a second propane canister for the grill. Alternatively, consider keeping a small tabletop charcoal grill in the attic along with enough charcoal to cook a week's worth of meals. In a pinch, you can even use wood in a charcoal grill.

GENERATORS

Generators can be invaluable during outages, but shopping for one can be overwhelming. Let's break down the major factors you should consider to make your decision a bit easier.

Generators come in a huge range of wattages, from small options to keep your phone, laptop, and router running to whole-house versions that will keep the fridge and HVAC working like normal. It may be helpful to pick up an inexpensive watt meter to check the actual wattage used by the items you'd like to power with your generator. I thought I had settled on a model for our home, thinking it could power our air fryer so we could use it in lieu of our oven during an outage. But when I checked, I found the air fryer uses way more wattage than I expected and I returned to the research stage.

There are a few questions to ask yourself to help decide which style of generator would be best for your home:

- How do you want your generator to be fueled?
- How much of your home do you want to be powered?
- How long do you plan to live in your current home?
- Do you want to be able to move the generator to different locations, like campsites or tailgating venues?

PORTABLE GENERATORS: Most portable generators run on gasoline and need to be regularly refueled (often more than once per day) if they are running constantly, powering something like a refrigerator. They are powerful and can be a huge asset, but keep in mind the refueling needs and their dependence on gasoline availability. These generators also need to stay outside for safety reasons and can be noisy. You'll need extension cords running into the house, or you can have an electrician connect the generator to your home's breaker box to cover a few of the outlets in your home. Portable generators are widely available in a range of wattages, so it's important to calculate your needs and choose a size suitable to your home.

POWER STATIONS: You could also choose a power station that holds power in a large battery and can be recharged with portable solar panels instead of refueled with gasoline. The power stations don't produce exhaust, so they can be used wherever needed within your home, including for CPAP machines overnight. They also come in a wide range of wattages, from small versions to keep your phone charged to models that can handle a refrigerator or television. Since they're not dependent on outside fuel, you'll be more self-sufficient if your yard gets enough sun. Look for models with large batteries so your generator will work longer without being recharged. The power stations are also chargeable in advance with a standard outlet, so you can have backup power ready to go all the time. If you do any camping or want a generator as part of your evacuation plan, this would be my choice because you don't need to transport fuel. The top wattage of solar-chargeable power stations is much lower than gas-powered generators, so there are still limitations with this option.

Solar solutions range from portable panels to whole-house systems.

WHOLE-HOUSE (STANDBY) GENERATORS: The ultimate solution for your home could be a whole-house generator, also called a standby generator, with an automatic transfer switch. These units are more permanently installed and tied directly to your home's electric panel, along with a connection to your natural gas or propane system. Because they're fueled directly through the pipes, you don't have to worry about going out to add gasoline regularly and they're always ready to kick into action. Like all the other options, whole-house generators come in a wide variety of wattages. A dealer can help choose one for the square footage of your home. The downside to this option is that it's more costly and not portable. It's an excellent option if you own your home and plan on staying for several years, but it may not make sense in other scenarios. There is also always a slight risk of interruption to your gas supply, which would prevent the generator from running.

SOLAR SOLUTION: Alternatively, you could switch your home to solar power if it's available in your area and not prohibited by your homeowner's association. Like whole-house generators, this option is most feasible if you own your home and won't be moving soon. The up-front cost can be high, but you'll benefit from lower utility bills year-round. As part of the system, it would be important to have a high-capacity battery to continue providing energy to your home on cloudy days. Often with solar power, your home is still connected to the grid, and the electric company provides supplemental power. Make sure you discuss options for higher levels of self-sufficiency when you're choosing a solar energy brand and configuration.

If you opt for a whole-house standby generator or whole-house solar solution, you can be more confident in adding more freezer space to expand your food storage.

Keep in mind that both gas and solar portable generators sell out very quickly in a disaster, while whole-house systems have long lead times before installation. It's important to be prepared before a disaster takes place, so you'll be able to create the optimal solution without compromising due to shortages.

If you opt for any of the generator options that don't connect to your HVAC system, do you need to pick up electric fans or space heaters to work with them? Make sure the wattages are compatible and consider that space heaters shouldn't be plugged into

Consider what wattage you need to work helpful appliances.

extension cords. Do you need lower-wattage versions of any kitchen appliances to run with your generator choice?

As you plan, you may find that a combination of generators is the right solution for your household. We realized it would be ideal to have a smaller solar-chargeable portable power station in the bedroom to keep the internet router functioning so we can work. It can also be used for recharging phones and laptops. This strategy is a good way to test out how well the portable solar panels in our backyard can recharge a unit on both sunny and cloudy days.

If it goes well, we'll invest in a higher-wattage unit for the kitchen that can power one of the refrigerators. In the meantime, before we upgrade to a larger model, I found a 200-watt mini rice cooker that will work with the small power station and provide an alternative to using the grill for any outages.

How to Store It All

Keep portable generators in an easy-to-access space in your garage. They should be tested and maintained as indicated in your owner's manual, and following those guidelines will be most likely when you don't have to move anything to access it. Gas-powered generators should be stored away from flammable items, including any chemicals, spray paint, or your hot-water heater if it's in the garage.

If you've purchased other small appliances to use with the generator that you won't use regularly, group them in a tote and add them to your garage or attic shelving with your other disaster supplies. Make sure the label clearly shows that the tote is for power outages so you can find it easily, even if you only have flashlight lighting.

Label each storage tote with the situation supplies it contains.

STEP 3: EXTENDED POWER OUTAGES

Extended power outages are challenging, especially when it comes to cooking, communication, and comfort. If you've opted for a generator as part of your step 2 plan, you may have adjusted relatively well to your new temporary lifestyle as an outage continues. Or, it may now be part of your normal routine to regularly pick up fresh ice for the cooler so you can keep refrigerator items on hand. Finding these new routines will help you mentally cope with longer periods without power.

Creative problem solving can also go a long way in staying comfortable. Is there a salon in another part of town with power where you can get a shampoo and blowout? While that may sound silly since hair can air-dry, looking and feeling like yourself can reduce stress, especially if you're still going to work or doing other activities outside your home.

In other situations, longer outages are a time to explore alternative housing until power is restored. You'll find more details for this scenario in Chapter 9, which covers evacuation. For widespread outages impacting stores as well as homes, you'll also want to consider the information in Chapter 8 covering loss of connectivity.

How many ways
does your household
use water each day?
Know your needs
and backup plan.

7

PREPARING
FOR LOSS
OF WATER

IN 2013, I EXPERIENCED THE "FUN" OF COMPROMISED WATER when my town's water supply was contaminated for a few days. Our water was still flowing, but it wasn't safe to use unless it was boiled. I quickly realized how much I've taken instant access to clean water for granted.

Luckily, most water outages are similar to what I experienced. The water is still flowing from faucets but can't be used as it normally would. But don't worry: even if your situation is more extreme, I'll also cover some preparations in case the water supply is completely interrupted.

STEP 1:
THE FIRST 72 HOURS

When there is any kind of water disruption, safe drinking water should be your first priority. Without it, your energy level will drop quickly, followed by more serious health effects. Beyond drinking, water is also essential for many other normal activities throughout the day.

What You Could Need

Experts recommend keeping 1 gallon of water per person per day on hand to cover drinking water and hygiene (like brushing teeth and washing hands). That means a

Calculate your water needs in advance, so there's no need to stress.

family of four should have a minimum of 12 gallons of water at home as their 72-hour water supply—four people times 3 days. Don't forget to add on extra water for your pets!

For your 72-hour supply, using purchased bottled water is the easiest option. We found 2.5-gallon jugs with built-in dispensers that work well for our water supply because they are rectangular. The shape means there is no wasted space when we store them. Five-gallon jugs to use with a water dispenser stand are a great option for larger families. While that may conjure a vision of your kitchen looking like a workplace, you may be surprised by some of the attractive stands now available. You can also get a pump that attaches directly to the top of the large jug to turn it into a faucet.

Once you have your water supply set for drinking, which will also cover brushing your teeth, your next thought might be how stinky everyone is going to be if you go 3 days without showering. Thankfully, we live in a world of convenience, and individually packaged waterless-shower body wipes are available in a variety of scents for men and women. They're marketed for both postworkout and camping convenience. Make sure you have enough for everyone in your home.

Stay fresh without water!

During a water outage, you will also need to stock items in the kitchen. Can you imagine what it would look and smell like if you couldn't rinse the dishes for 3 days? As soon as you know there is a problem with the water, start using as many disposable items as possible. Plates, bowls, and silverware made from bamboo rather than plastic can reduce the environmental impact from disposables. Don't forget coffee cups! Depending on the nature of the water advisory, if your dishwasher heats water to 150°F, it may still be safe to use. Your water company and health department should release specific guidance at the time of the emergency for exactly which household activities are safe and which should be avoided.

During a water outage is a great time to grill meat and veggies outside without getting pots and pans dirty inside. As you decide what to eat, consider how much water the actual meal needs and how many dirty dishes the preparation will take.

Stock up on hand sanitizer with at least 60 percent alcohol, and use it instead of water when your hands are not visibly dirty. This will also help stretch your water supply.

While your toilet will still function normally if the water is contaminated, in the event of a total water outage, you'll have to manually flush your toilets or find an alternative bathroom option. To manually flush, you'll need some rainwater or another water source and a bucket that holds 1 gallon of water. Dump the full gallon into the toilet bowl at once, which will cause the toilet to flush.

Opt for hand sanitizer when you can to conserve water.

Since the manual flushing option still requires a water source, consider keeping a camping toilet or commode in your storage area, along with a stockpile of compostable waste bags to line the inside. To make this process as pleasant as possible, you should also keep a waste gelling product with your emergency toilet. The magical mix turns liquids into gel for less mess and, perhaps more importantly, deodorizes any waste.

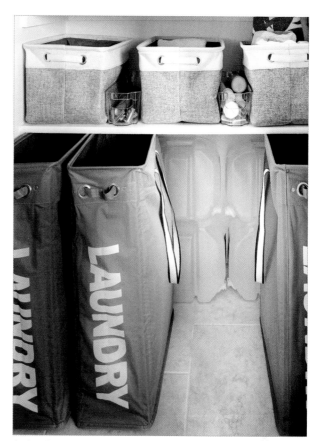
Go low for water storage.

How to Store It All

Water is the bulkiest item to store, and few people have room within their kitchen for 3 days' worth of water for their household. You don't want plastic exposed to heat, so garages and attics are not a good option. If you have a pantry, consider storing water on the floor below the bottom shelf. Closet floors in general are the best option because it keeps the heavy water containers on the ground, minimizing damage if they were ever to leak. If you have any deep closets, try keeping water on the floor in the back, with more frequently used items in front. For example, behind the clothes hampers in our master bathroom closet, I can conceal 10 gallons of water without it impacting the function of the space. The space on the floor of bedroom closets, under hanging items, can also work well for water storage. Only stack your water bottles if the plastic is firm enough not to shift or indent at all. We learned the hard way that any motion in the plastic can turn into cracks over time.

In Chapter 9, which covers evacuation, we'll be putting together emergency backpacks. We keep our showerless body wipes in those backpacks so we can still shower on the go, but they double as an item we'd using during a water outage.

For the disposable kitchenware, you may always have a 3-day supply stored with your normal party supplies. If not, start a tote for your emergency shelving labeled "Water Outage: Kitchen."

If you've opted to add a camping toilet, I recommend keeping it in a storage tote, along with your waste bags and gel. The tote can also be stored on your emergency shelving in the garage, attic, or basement.

Simple, labeled totes can store everything you need.

STEP 2: PREPARING FOR 10 DAYS

For some homes, it would be impossible to effectively store enough water for 10 days. If you have the room, go ahead and increase your water stockpile to last that duration. But if you can't, let's look at some alternative methods you can use.

What You Could Need

Always keep extra coffee filters on hand for filtering water as well.

According to the FEMA/Red Cross guide *Food and Water in an Emergency*, boiling water is the most effective way to kill microorganisms, so keeping a large pot on hand to prepare drinkable water is a good idea. Before boiling, you may need to remove any solid contaminants, which is most easily done with a coffee filter. Once you've filtered the water, make sure it maintains a rolling boil for at least 1 minute. To improve the taste of boiled or stored water, you can add oxygen by pouring the water back and forth between two containers before drinking.

If boiling isn't an option, water purification tablets can be used to purify water in under an hour. They neutralize bacteria and parasites and are commonly used by hikers. A company called LifeStraw has created straws and water bottles with two integrated filters to make water from nature instantly safe to drink. Be sure to read the instructions for priming the filters before use and consider ordering some replacement filters as well.

If a water outage is an isolated problem, you'll still be able to grocery shop for meals that don't require water for preparation or even dine out if restaurants aren't impacted. However, if a water outage happens in conjunction with a larger emergency, you may have to get creative with meals. Pause and look at the menu you created in the earlier chapters.

Disposables help you save wash water for more important uses.

How many of them can be made without water? While standbys like rice, pasta, and oatmeal are great in most scenarios, they're not ideal when water isn't easily available.

Keep some disposable aluminum pans with your other disposable kitchenware so you don't have to wash pots and pans. Your grill will come in handy—you can cook directly on the grates or in foil packets. Reynolds even makes a heavy-duty nonstick foil specifically for grilling. Premade pizza crusts also work without a pan, either on your grill with indirect heat or directly on your oven grates. Let each family member assemble their own pizza to add a little entertainment and fun to your waterless evening.

Make sure your meal list includes choices like freezer meals that only need to be reheated, as well as foods that can be prepared if the power is also out. While dehydrated soups are tasty and save storage space for stay-at-home planning, you should also have some ready-to-eat canned soup and chili as options that are both shelf-stable and easily reheated on a grill or camp stove without water or electricity. Heat them in one of your disposable aluminum pans. They're not shaped like a traditional soup pot but will do the job. Just be very cautious when transporting the disposable pans since they aren't solid and you could be burned if the contents spill. Canned vegetables and tuna or chicken are

ALTERNATIVE WATER SOURCES

Options for purifying water for drinking are great, but if the supply is stopped altogether, where can you find the water to purify?

If you can find a moving river or stream, that's an ideal water source. Lakes and large ponds are other alternatives. If you're not familiar with any running streams, rivers, or lakes near your home, you should locate and visit at least two options and note the locations in the Family Plan section of your preparedness binder.

If you have a pool or spa, the water shouldn't be used for drinking, but can be used for hygiene and toilet flushing.

Do you have a tank-style hot-water heater? If so, it should be full of water that you can access by attaching a hose to the drain at the bottom. Print out a copy of the instructions for draining your model and add it to your preparedness binder.

You can use rain barrels in the backyard to gather water, but keep in mind that rainwater can be contaminated by microparticles from your roof shingles. It's still a valuable resource for toilet flushing, though. You can also set up a rainwater collection system using one of your tarps and cording from your emergency repair bin.

Rainwater can keep toilets flushing.

also good bets for electricity-free, water-free meals.

Stock up on additional shower wipes and disposable kitchenware to get you through 10 days without water. My mind always defaults to dinner when I'm calculating what we'll need in the kitchen, so if you have that same tendency, this is your official reminder to count what each person will need for breakfast and lunch as well.

How to Store It All

We keep our LifeStraw bottles attached to our emergency backpacks so they'll be handy if we ever need to evacuate. Each backpack also contains a bottle of water purification tabs—the

Bamboo reduces the enviromental impact of disposables.

bottles are small and light, so it's worth having two options for water purification. Extra purification tabs and bottle filters can be placed in your water emergency bin with the toilet supplies.

While 3 days of disposable kitchenware can be stored with your regular party supplies, once you get beyond that, it's good to keep it separate to save prime kitchen space and to make sure you always have enough. If you didn't start a bin for your disposable kitchen items in the last step, create one now. If you're in an extremely hot environment, it's always wise to do an occasional check to make sure nothing has melted.

STEP 3: EXTENDED LOSS OF WATER

In all but the most extreme, unprecedented scenarios, water would have been restored, bottled water would be available, or water trucks would have arrived to support your community before a water outage got beyond 10 days.

Keep empty bottles on hand to refill until you're confident your water supply is back again.

Keep in mind that even if bottled water becomes available for drinking and cooking, storing a larger supply of disposable products will help reduce your water usage until the normal supply returns. Calculate how many plates, cups, bowls, and utensils your family would need and add them to your kitchen water outage bin.

Make sure that everyone keeps the large empty bottles of water you have on hand at the beginning of a water outage. You may need to refill them with water to be filtered, and the more bottles you have, the fewer times you'll have to visit your water source to fill them.

Before you lose access,
consider how to live offline
in comfort and safety.

8

PREPARING FOR LOSS OF CONNECTIVITY

OUR WORLD NOW DEPENDS ON RELIABLE INTERNET service and electronics more than ever. When our service at home has temporary outages, we're frustrated by the simple things, like not being able to access our email and Netflix. Usually, we can still access websites through our phones, so the overall impact is an annoyance rather than a serious situation.

However, widespread cyberattacks on vital internet services, infrastructure attacks using electromagnetic pulse (EMP), or solar superstorms creating geomagnetic disturbance (GMD) could each be devastating. The last major GMD event was in 1989 and caused six million people in Quebec to lose power for up to 9 hours. At that time, overall infrastructure depended less on electronics and connectivity than it does now. There is still some disagreement over how we would be impacted today and how long it would take to restore services. There's also disagreement over the likelihood of an EMP attack as many believe the threat of a US nuclear response is a sufficient deterrent. The Department of Homeland Security has a task force dedicated to mitigating risks of an EMP attack. It is working on plans to put redundancies in place to limit any effects of either man-made or natural impacts to our overall infrastructure in the future.

In the meantime, with almost every facet of our life relying on electronics of some kind, there are a few extra challenges to plan for in this chapter, some of which are very simple to overcome and some of which may feel a bit scarier. Just remember that putting the resources in place now will make it so much easier for you to stay calm if we're ever confronted with a major technology outage.

Make sure your communication, navigation, financial access, and other connections extend beyond a few powered devices.

STEP 1:
THE FIRST 72 HOURS

What if you had no access to your finances during the outage? Transactions using credit and debit cards run through the internet. Most modern cash registers require online access, so while cash is a better bet, many stores wouldn't be prepared to check you out manually.

Does your work rely on internet access? Because I'm self-employed and all my income streams are online, my income would immediately drop to zero. If you're in a similar situation, increase your savings accordingly.

The good news in this chapter is that you've done most of the work already if you've implemented the steps in the other chapters. Because you're fully prepared to stay at home, even without water or electricity, you're in great shape to hunker down until all the brilliant minds and dedicated workers in our country restore functionality. You shouldn't need access to your funds initially because you already have everything you need at home.

What You Could Need

Let's start with a quick, easy fix. If your meal plan relies on any recipes you access online, print them out now and add them to your binder. Include recipes for foods you normally buy but can make from scratch if necessary, like hamburger or hot dog buns. Look through any cookbooks you have at home to see if they cover meals you can make with your pantry staples or if your collection includes more elaborate recipes with special ingredients that you don't keep on hand. For example, if your child or spouse has a birthday during this outage, it would be great to have a simple cake and frosting recipe in one of your cookbooks. I think this might even call for a trip to a local bookstore to grab a coffee and browse through the cookbook section.

Our TV runs through the internet, so if it was down, along with our cell phones, we'd be most frightened by not knowing what caused the event. If that happens to you, check your weather radio for information in case radio signals are still successfully being broadcast.

Walkie-talkies could be a communication channel in an emergency.

As you think about your communication needs, consider redundancy in your plans. Do you want a landline phone for emergencies that impact the cell towers? What about walkie-talkies for communication with family? If you add walkie-talkies, remember to make a plan for recharging them. A set that could be used with a solar-charging power station could be ideal so you don't have to worry about batteries. Ham radios are the most reliable type of backup communication, but they do require a simple license to operate. Make sure to check government guidelines if you are interested in that option.

File paper records of contact information.

In the Contacts section of your preparedness binder, create a list of everyone you may want to reach in a disaster, including their address and phone number. You should already have doctors, insurance agents, and lawyers covered in the appropriate sections, but how many addresses and phone numbers of friends and family members do you know by heart? What about numbers for employers, schools, and utility companies? Make yourself a personalized phone book for your binder to use in case you need to travel to a contact's home location or landline phones are restored before cellular devices and online access.

How to Store It All

Good news: you don't need to store much for this step because you've already done all the work of gathering and storing food and household supplies in prior chapters!

If you don't have a designated space for cookbooks, do what I do. I love keeping most of ours out as part of our kitchen décor. They live between bookends on the shelving in the kitchen nook. If that won't work and you don't have free space in the pantry, add them to any bookcase or cube organizer in the house.

If you've decided to bolster your communication channels with walkie-talkies, keep them in your emergency backpack or storm shelter so they'll always be handy. A ham radio can stay with your power outage supplies.

Keep print recipes handy.

STEP 2: PREPARING FOR 10 DAYS

This is a tricky disaster to plan for because no one knows for sure how long it would take to get various systems back online. The most likely reality is that although everything shut down at once, we'd get access to each service back at different times. It wouldn't be like one national light switch turned off and then back on. Instead, many cities and service providers would be working to bring everything back to fully functioning. You may see water, lights, and internet all come back separately and in a different order than a family member in another town experiences.

Gas pumps also need power, so you may not be able to refuel your cars or generator. Unfortunately, because some households won't have adequate preparations to stay at home and because security systems won't be functional, civil disobedience would be likely, similar to what is seen after devastating hurricanes. This makes it even more important for you to be prepared to stay safely at home and away from businesses or crowded areas. However, if you reside in an area experiencing crime, evacuation may become necessary and you can rely on the tips in the next chapter.

If the impact is limited to your area and you have family in another region that you could stay with, you'll need to navigate to them without GPS.

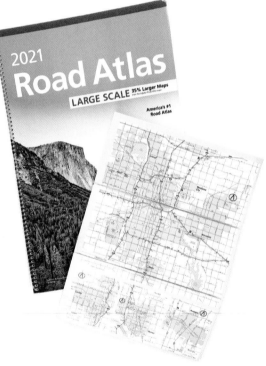

If GPS is unavailable, could you read a map?

What You Could Need

If you don't already have one, order an updated national road atlas, plus a good state map and a compass. Because GPS satellites can be impacted, if you rely on Google Maps or Waze for each trip out of town, you need a backup plan.

In the early 2000s, before GPS units were widely available and when our cell phones were purely phones, I drove my boss and a coworker 2 hours west to Oklahoma City for a meeting. Before heading home, we wanted to pay our respects at the new Oklahoma City National Memorial that opened after the Murrah Federal Building bombing. None of us were familiar with downtown Oklahoma City, and we learned quickly that I was the only one in the car who could read a map, despite my passengers being very intelligent people. After their unsuccessful attempts at map reading, we needed to pull over in an unknown area so I could safely see the map and get us back on track.

These days, even fewer people can navigate with a printed map. It's understandable because they've never needed to! I don't want you to find yourself stressed about map navigation if GPS is unavailable, so I added a fun challenge for you in the box below.

NAVIGATION CHALLENGE

Once your new road atlas and state maps have arrived, pick a location in your state that you've never visited but would enjoy for a day trip. It could be a state park, a restaurant in another town, or anything that sounds fun to you. Just make sure you select somewhere outside your normal stomping grounds so it's a bit of a challenge.

Work with a copilot to navigate to your destination without using your phone. On the way home, the driver and navigator should swap places so each gets a turn with the map.

If you have older kids, plan a trip to multiple locations so they can learn as well. Just remember that this activity is fun and you should be patient with any wrong turns. And make sure you have a full tank of gas before setting out!

Does your bank have an offline backup of records to allow you access to your funds if they are disconnected? Talk to your bank about its emergency procedures, but also keep cash for any unexpected necessities at home. Smaller bills are important because you don't want to be stuck with only hundred-dollar bills when you're trying to buy small necessities if some stores, or even local farms, are able to accept cash.

How to Store It All

Keep the maps in your vehicle so they're always handy in an emergency. My phone once overheated and turned off while I was navigating and wouldn't reconnect to the map for almost an hour. Luckily, I knew I was just driving north for quite a while, but I wished I had an emergency map in the car to double-check the next highway I needed to take.

Keep any emergency cash in a safe place within the house, because the odds of a house fire are higher than this more extreme scenario. I picked up the fire- and water-safe envelopes shown at right for cash and our most important documents, like passports. Then, those envelopes are kept inside the fire safe for a second layer of protection. Plan to quickly grab the pouch and add it to your backpack in the event of an evacuation.

Protect your cash and important documents at home and on the go.

STEP 3: EXTENDED LOSS OF CONNECTIVITY

No one knows exactly what would happen to our financial system if there was an extended outage. If I dwell on that thought, it's easy to stir up panic. So, instead, I think about the innovative people who have made wild ideas come to life over the past decade. We couldn't have imagined carrying a tiny computer in our pocket that makes phone calls, has multiple cameras that take professional-quality photos, and connects us to the entire world while also letting us preorder coffee customized precisely to our tastes.

I think this same technological innovation will help us overcome future challenges in ways we can't even anticipate now. New companies will pop up with creative solutions to pressing problems. This makes it feel more manageable to be as prepared as we can for a longer total outage without letting fear take over. We choose to be prepared to stay home several months until hard work and innovation restore some normalcy, and to trust that the restoration will happen. Otherwise, for us, the trade-off is too great. We'd be spending our limited time on earth always concerned about what-ifs and worst-case scenarios instead of embracing all the goodness and joy that is possible.

While that's our approach, it's important for you to set your own. Maybe you feel the opposite and can't relax unless you have a full multiyear stockpile. As long as you're not letting it overwhelm your home and you're still making time to enjoy other activities, that's great too.

What You Could Need

With longer outages, we can look to tumultuous times in history for some tips on surviving more comfortably. In addition to cash, gold can be an asset. Historically, jewelry has also been valuable to have for trade-in during devastating times. I'm not going to argue with a win-win gift of something beautiful to wear now that can double as emergency currency.

If you run low on important items before the outage is resolved, bartering with neighbors is a good option. There are differing opinions on how to approach the potential for bartering. For example, some people would give you almost anything for cigarettes, so people stockpile cigarettes. My approach is to stick to items we could actually use ourselves, but I keep a bit more beyond what I think we would need.

Simple, but essential, items like trash bags, toilet paper, and soap will be sought by those who weren't prepared. Because they don't expire, I can keep extra on hand without worrying about waste. As we use the items in normal life, I restock them, so we'll always have extra if needed.

Whatever you choose to barter, having a good relationship with your neighbors in advance of a disaster will be helpful. It can become complicated quickly if they aren't prepared, and emotionally difficult if you want to help them but can't spare food your family needs. To find a supply buddy to trade with first, consider someone else nearby who you know also has a stockpile.

Protecting your home may be a concern if resources aren't available and others become desperate. If you choose to own a firearm, make sure you have adequate ammunition, everyone in your home has attended a safety course, and it's not accessible to children. Whether or not you opt to own a firearm, you should still make a plan for how to handle a home invasion. If you have a storm shelter, can it become a safe place if you hear someone trying to break in? While you don't want to have your supplies stolen, your life is more important.

If part of your food plan includes activities like gardening and canning your harvest, would that plan be hindered if you couldn't read tips and instructions online? Consider investing in printed books about any new skills you may need to learn in an emergency. Along with cookbooks, I have a couple of gardening guides to give me the best chance of a successful backyard crop, including starting with seeds of any fresh vegetables we have on hand.

Installing a wall safe could be your next home-improvement project.

How to Store It All

Any gold or other jewelry can be kept in a home safe. While documents are generally fine in a portable safe, consider installing a more secure wall or floor safe for valuables. Many wall safes are designed to be easily placed between studs, and the fronts are often flat enough that they can be concealed behind artwork.

Extra bartering items can be stored wherever you keep your regular stockpile of that item. For example, all of our hand soap is grouped together in a guest bathroom and soap for showering is all in our master linen closet. If inside space is at a premium, you could add a bartering bin to your disaster shelving instead.

I know this whole chapter has a bit of a science fiction feel, and it's hard to envision a day when everything connected electronically instantly stops working. I was relieved to work through what that would mean and realized that while we were preparing for the more understood disasters, like weather events and pandemics, we had done most of the prep for this situation as well. Because a large-scale attack or solar storm could take months of recovery, consider increasing your supply goals for food, water, and household items once you've met your initial targets for each chapter.

Make it easier for everyone to leave your home when needed.

9

WHEN YOU CAN'T STAY IN YOUR HOME

YOU MADE IT TO THE LAST DISASTER PLANNING STEP! Throughout most of the book, we prepared everything you'll need to be able to stay safely, comfortably, and stylishly at home in almost any circumstance. Staying home has many advantages, including access to all your supplies, but in certain circumstances, it could become safer to leave.

In this final section, you'll pull things together for the rare situations in which evacuation is the best option. By making evacuation plans in advance, you'll be less frantic if an evacuation is ordered and less likely to forget anything important when you go. The chapter will also help you think through where you would go in the event of an evacuation. If you have pets that will be leaving with you, it's especially important to track down pet-friendly options in advance.

HOW TO PREPARE NOW

In the Evacuation section of your binder, outline at least three choices of evacuation location. As you do this, make sure your options are located in different directions from your home. For example, you may choose a family member's house that is in another town west of your home, a hotel in a small town a few hours north, and a friend's house to the south. Make sure you have the phone numbers of each location, and at least two routes to each spot that you can navigate to without GPS.

For each location, make notes about why you chose it and when it would be most appropriate. For example, if there was a widespread natural disaster in my area, we could stay at a friend's house in Denver until services were restored in our town. In other scenarios, I would avoid going to a larger city or welcome her family to our home. It may seem silly to write out these evacuation plans now, but it's easier to think clearly and make better decisions when you're not in the middle of a stressful situation.

The other important additions to your binder will be two versions of a list of items to take with you. The first should be a shorter list of everything you need to grab during an evacuation with very little warning. The second should have all the short-list items plus anything you want to add when you have time to plan in advance. For example, if a wildfire or hurricane is moving toward your home, but the evacuation zone may or may not reach you, you can be proactive and start gathering items in advance just in case.

As you create your quick evacuation and evacuation with warning lists, consider breaking each one into sections for each household member. When each person knows what they're in charge of, there will be less chaos as you try to get everything packed into the car. It may be helpful to note the location within the house of any specific senti-mental items on the list. This is especially important in case the person who makes the list isn't home when an evacuation is ordered.

Create a "go" plan with three safe locations, then assign packing tasks.

EVACUATING TO A SHELTER, HOTEL, OR ANOTHER HOME

During evacuations caused by natural disasters, it's likely that within a few hours' drive you can be somewhere unaffected. If you don't have family or friends to stay with, pick out a few options for preferred hotels in advance. You don't want to be obsessing over online reviews and trying to make a hotel decision at the last minute when you could have the decision made ahead of time. Make reservations the moment you think evacuation could be a possibility—rooms can fill quickly. Before choosing hotels, consider any essential features plus things that would make your stay more comfortable. We'd

Think about any special accommodations you might need, such as pet-friendly lodging.

need somewhere that was dog-friendly and would prefer if it also had a kitchenette. For any stays that would be more than a few days, on-site laundry services would be a big help. You might not need a pet-friendly hotel but may have a gym or indoor pool on your must-have list.

If you have a vacation home within drivable range from your main home, it could be your perfect backup plan. Stock the kitchen with pantry staples and water and the bathrooms with your usual toiletries. Consider adding solar panels or a generator for backup power. We dream of owning our own cabin or lake house in the future. Finding a beautiful spot to relax on the weekends, which could also be a self-sufficient space during a major disaster, would be ideal.

What You Could Need

The first thing to grab before evacuating should be your preparedness binder. Not only will you use it as you pack, but you also need to take it with you when you leave. Each section has details that could come in handy while you are away from home.

Your evacuation checklist should include your passports and cash from your safe. Gather them right after your binder.

"Go bags" or "bug out bags" are popular terms for items gathered together in a backpack for an instant evacuation. Because they are generally for worst-case scenarios and full of survival gear, they could be overkill for an evacuation to a hotel, a friend's house, or even an emergency shelter. For example, I won't need tarps at a hotel. Instead, I'd probably want my laptop and charger. With that in mind, we've modified this concept a bit. We do have one shared, extreme evacuation bag that I'll talk about in the next section, but we use a different approach for the more likely evacuation scenario in which we'd still have access to food, water, and power.

During normal travel, we use packing cubes to keep things organized and to maximize what fits in each suitcase. These same cubes make packing for an evacuation more efficient. Instead of unpacking my travel-sized toiletries after each trip, they stay in a

> ## HONORING YOUR OWN TERMS
>
> I spent a lot of time avoiding any type of disaster preparation because my impression was that being prepared involved not only food and water taking over the house, but also camping in the wilderness. And not the kind of "camping" I enjoy, which includes fully functioning cabins with kitchens and laundry rooms. Everything changed when I realized that staying at home was almost always the best, that we could prepare and still have a beautifully organized home, and that evacuating to another space with indoor plumbing is almost always an option. It would be only the most extreme, unprecedented circumstances that would cause us to head for the forest. Those are terms I can handle!

cube, so it's always ready to go. In addition to storing basics like body wash, deodorant, and toothpaste, I keep a week's worth of prescription medication and a spare pair of disposable contacts in the cube. Anything I'd consider my bare-minimum necessities for an overnight trip away from home is always ready to go. Because I travel with these items regularly, I just replenish them as needed and know that the products are still good.

The second technique that would help me pack quickly in the event of a sudden evacuation is a customized packing list. I was tired of constantly fearing I would forget something when traveling and sick of lying awake at night days before a flight, making mental checklists. Creating my packing list has been a huge stress reducer. It's a printed checklist of every single item I may need, for any type of travel. I keep copies of the list in a folder, so it's easy to grab the paper and check things off as I pack. Of course, not everything is needed for each trip, so my first satisfying task is marking off whatever doesn't apply.

That packing list forms the basis of my evacuation packing list, with nonrelevant items removed. (I sure hope I never need a strapless bra in an emergency!) In addition to writing down the items I need for myself, I listed all the items we'd need to pack for the dogs. By preparing to pack quickly instead of prepacking, we can adjust our clothing to be more weather appropriate. This is especially important in climates that vary seasonally. Some months, you could need thermal underwear and wool socks, while others could call for shorts and sandals. We can also adjust the number of outfits we pack based on the emergency, if we have an idea whether we'll be gone for a few nights or a longer period.

Because this process does still require some packing time, it won't hurt to start packing early if you learn that there is even a remote chance of evacuation.

Think through and add to your list any other items your family would require beyond clothing and toiletries if you needed to leave your home. This could include practical items like phone chargers and comfort items like your favorite pillow. While food should be available for purchase in your alternate location, consider bringing favorite snacks, beverages, and even some meal items if you'll be using a hotel kitchenette. Breakfast foods are nice to have on hand in hotels, especially if you have kids who get up early and wake up hungry. What about entertainment? A deck of cards or other small games can help beat boredom and reduce screen time.

How to Store It All

For anything that can be packed in advance, like the toiletry packing cube I mentioned earlier, pack it now and store it inside your most-used suitcase. Additionally, you could give yourself a head start before any trip by keeping a packing cube of undergarments ready to go in the same suitcase. My luck would be that the week I was behind on laundry, we'd have an unexpected disaster and be short on clean socks and underwear.

WORST-CASE SCENARIO: EVACUATING TO AN ISOLATED AREA

While this book focuses on the most common disasters and how to be prepared to thrive through them at home, most disaster preppers focus on how to survive a more apocalyptic event, like total societal breakdown that makes leaving your home and staying away from any populated area the safest option. The somewhat reassuring news is that even as advanced nations like England and France endured both World Wars within their borders, including in huge cities like London that were bombed, most citizens remained in their homes or with friends outside targeted areas. That doesn't mean it was easy. Supply shortages and food rationing went on well after the war ended. Reading historically accurate fiction novels set in those times has been a great inspiration for me to prepare our home.

Because our focus in this book is on preparing to stay at home and not extreme survival, I'm not going to get into details but want to lightly touch on things to consider keeping on hand to take with you during a worst-case scenario.

Determine Escape Locations

First, decide where you would go. There's often a vague notion of escaping to the woods, but what does that really look like? You don't want to trespass on anyone's property, and national forests could be popular if everyone has the same idea. Brainstorm options, including some closer to home and others farther outside your area. Make a list of your possible camping areas and add them to your binder. If you don't have a vehicle and live in a larger city, know at least two locations you would head toward and two ways to get to them. Collaborate with friends who live or work near you to travel together when possible.

Plan Water and Food

When planning an extreme evacuation, your biggest concerns will be water, food, and shelter. Most of the items in your emergency bag should relate to those concepts. For water, look back to the options in Chapter 7 on preparing for loss of water, and make sure you have at least two different ways to make water safe to drink. Keep everything you need for both methods in your bag. We don't keep duplicates of items like our LifeStraw bottles; instead, they're stored in our evacuation bags all the time. For basic hygiene, include at least a 3-day supply of showerless wipes along with some waterless disposable toothbrushes. Condensed rolls of camping toilet paper are a much more comfortable choice than relying on leaves, and they save room in your pack.

As with water, you have a head start on your food for evacuation as well. Remember when you planned what to eat if you had to stay home with no water and no electricity? Those are the same items you'll want to pack in your emergency bag. Each person needs at least a 72-hour supply of food in the backpack. Instead of keeping all your flavored

Focus your supplies on water, food, and shelter.

tuna packets in the pantry, keep some in the emergency backpack. Set a repeating reminder on your calendar to check the food quarterly and rotate it out to prevent spoilage. Toss a small lightweight can opener in your bag, even if you're not using any canned items. If they become available in trade or through a rationing program, you'll need an easy way to open them.

Secure Shelter

Now that you have water and food covered, you need to stay warm and dry. Lightweight tents are a good option, but you could also create a DIY shelter between trees with paracord and a tarp. Paracord is a lightweight rope made up of 32 braided strands of nylon, which make it extremely strong.

In addition to the large tarps, Mylar emergency blankets can keep you warm, and they're extremely small and lightweight to carry. They can also double as groundcover or tenting in a pinch.

CREATING A CAR KIT

Create an emergency car kit and keep it in your vehicle at all times. The kit won't just be for major evacuations; it may come in handy for a range of small emergencies, even a cut finger while tailgating. The following items are recommended:

- Cell phone charger
- Car fire extinguisher
- First-aid kit—including any vital medication
- Flashlight and batteries (Consider headlamp-style.)
- Tire pressure gauge
- Tire inflator and sealant
- Jumper cables or battery-powered jump-start device
- Road atlas and compass
- Water bottle and purification tabs
- Mylar emergency blankets
- Shelf-stable food items like trail mix and jerky (Rotate these so they're eaten before expiring.)
- Warning triangles
- LED flares
- Ice scraper
- Duct tape
- Change and small bills for toll roads

Know how to access and install your spare tire, and confirm that all the parts are in good working order. A pipe that fits over the lug wrench handle can help create valuable leverage if strength is a concern. If you've never changed a tire, head to the driveway and practice so it's less intimidating if you have to do it in the future on the side of the road.

While one of the supplies in your car kit will help you purify water in an emergency, it's also a good idea to pack extra bottled water when you're traveling more than just around town, in case you're ever stranded on the road.

Since we have an SUV, plan A for me would be laying down the back seats and using sleeping bags in the car. Any supplies that wouldn't fit in the car while we were sleeping could go on the roof, covered with a tarp to stay dry and protected. In fact, if it was raining, putting a tarp over the car would allow us to open the windows for ventilation but still keep the inside dry.

Gather Other Helpful Supplies

Add at least two pairs of thick wool socks per person to help prevent blisters and keep feet warm and dry, and don't forget extra underwear. For clothing, lightweight rain suits that fit over your clothing are a good choice in addition to a change of clothes and shoes appropriate for hiking.

You'll want at least two options to start fires, which is important for warmth in the winter and cooking year-round. Learning how to use a ferro rod with a striker is a great waterproof option in addition to matches. Ferro rods are made out of a special alloy that creates extremely hot sparks when struck with another piece of metal. The sparks can then start kindling for a fire. A multipurpose survival knife is also essential—make sure it can cut both your paracord and branches if necessary. Keep one of your portable phone chargers and a solar rechargeable radio/flashlight device in the bag for news updates, communication, and light.

A POWER COUPLE

Paracord and tarps together have many other uses beyond shelter. For instance, they can be rigged to catch rainwater. The cording alone can be used as is or unbraided into thinner rope to create everything from shoelaces to fishing line.

Worth the investment!

With your water, food, and shelter covered in your emergency bag and additional helpful items like the first-aid kit in your vehicle all the time, you should be able to stay reasonably comfortable in the short-term, first 72 hours of an emergency evacuation. This planning will meet the government's recommendations, and hopefully none of us will ever need to escape for a longer period.

If you choose to prepare for a longer period away, consider gathering additional items in a storage tote that can be quickly moved to the car. Because we have the small solar-rechargeable generator, I'd add that to our list, along with additional food and cooking supplies. You can also create a full wish list of everything you'd want to pack if you had to evacuate to an isolated location for a longer period of time. Add this to your binder, and then aim to start packing the items in the car early if any current events lead you to believe evacuation will become a serious option. There are many great survivalist resources with more detailed suggestions for go bags and living off the land if that is a direction in which you'd like to take your preparedness.

Stay ahead of any situation by focusing on what you can control in any given week.

NEXT STEPS: LIVING BEAUTIFULLY PREPARED, NOT PANICKED

IN THE BEGINNING OF THIS BOOK, I TALKED ABOUT THE IMPORTANCE OF BALANCING your acts of preparedness with your normal life. Going forward, continue to remind yourself of that equilibrium. We could make ourselves crazy trying to account for every unknown. Instead, try to reframe your planning into living beautifully prepared, not panicked. Don't let what could happen in the future steal your peace today. Instead, take the steps to help your household thrive in a variety of situations and then step back into enjoying life.

As you do that, there are a few final tips that I hope make both your everyday life and emergencies a bit easier.

First, focus on the things you can control. You can't stop the unpredictable nature of life, but by planning ahead and not getting behind on weekly tasks, you'll also be ahead in case of a disaster. If your laundry is always behind, that situation creates an immediate problem if there is a water outage. Sticking to a schedule that helps you stay on top of the laundry will reduce the normal stress each time you see an overflowing hamper, plus it ensures you can thrive without water for a longer period before clean clothing or towels become a concern. The same concept applies to the dishes. If we lost water, I'd want that to happen while the sink was empty and not full, so we try to keep the sink empty. It's possible that we'll never have a major water outage, but I still benefit from staying on top of the dishes each time I walk in and see the clean kitchen.

Mentally focusing on things within your control can also help in your planning. Try to catch yourself if your mind starts dwelling on "what if" scenarios or you begin feeling anxious. Instead of thinking how horrible any particular disaster would be, switch your thoughts to the parts you can control. For example, if you find yourself concerned about a fire, think about actions you can take to prevent your property from being impacted by a fire plus anything you could do to make a fire less devastating, like scanning old photos into a cloud-based storage.

If you don't already have a good relationship with your neighbors, spend time getting to know them. When you can work together during a disaster, everyone benefits. Find a few you connect with the most, and make sure their phone numbers are in the Contacts section of your binder. These relationships will also come in handy well before an emergency. While we had mostly waved at neighbors when we lived in our first home, we now have a '50s-sitcom relationship with the couple next door. Before we had our own stockpile, milk, sugar, and ice had all been exchanged in both directions over the years, sometimes passed over the back fence. It's now a Thanksgiving tradition that I borrow extra glass baking dishes from them, and we have access to each other's

Sharing supplies is a smart strategy.

Working with your neighbors can help you both get through the everyday tough stuff and beyond.

homes to let our dogs out as needed. Entertaining is a great motivation to spruce up the house, so inviting neighbors over for dinner or drinks can help you stay on top of housework while building relationships.

Striking a balance between adding to your stockpile and keeping the house decluttered is also important. Our closets were full of stuff before, but it wasn't always things that added value to our lives. Much of it was random items we had acquired over the last 20 years and no longer used. Going through the process of creating our home stockpile made me more willing to let go of items that we don't need, which prevents the house from getting overloaded and cluttered. It also made me more intentional with what we bring into our house because I'm more aware that every item will have to be stored somewhere. I hope you'll experience the same results.

Stay aware of the weather and other news. Following your regional National Weather Service branch is a great way to get a no-hype heads-up before any storms. Because conditions can change quickly, check for updates regularly so you can adjust your plans if needed. For example, as I write this final chapter, our portable power station is plugged in to make sure it's fully charged. Throughout the day, it's been cold and raining, but we were supposed to stay above freezing and avoid the ice accumulation and power outages already seen to our west. With each updated forecast, the freeze zone has worked its way closer to our home. I plugged in the power station just in case, and since then, we've been officially added to the winter weather advisory.

Check for updates regularly.

Despite the warning, I have nothing else to do to get ready. I don't have to bundle up and go out in the almost-freezing rain to get groceries because we're already stocked with everything we need, even if we lose power. I don't need to hurry through washing towels because they're already clean based on our normal schedule. Our candles and flashlights

Stay prepared by keeping all critical devices powered up.

Even if you never need to use your plans, you will be rewarded with everyday calm!

are ready, along with extra blankets. Instead of being stressed by a changing forecast and winter storm coming much earlier in the season than we normally experience, I'm cozy in the house and can relax with a book this evening, knowing we're prepared.

The calm I feel now is what I dream of for you. It's exactly why I wanted to write this book. Despite endless advances in technology meant to make our lives easier, things feel busier and more stressful than ever. A home that beautifully reflects your style while also holding everything you need to thrive in an emergency creates the perfect place for you to recharge. When we have a space that helps us feel at peace, we can be our best. And when we're our best, everyone benefits. Keep your focus on the goal of having a beautifully prepared home, and I think you'll love the results.

INDEX